Where t

Wind Dreams

of Staying

SEARCHING FOR

PURPOSE AND PLACE

IN THE WEST

Eric Dieterle

Oregon State University Press | Corvallis

Library of Congress Cataloging-in-Publication Data

Names: Dieterle, Eric, author.
Title: Where the wind dreams of staying : searching for purpose and place in the West / Eric Dieterle.
Other titles: Searching for purpose and place in the West
Description: Corvallis : Oregon State University Press, 2016.
Identifiers: LCCN 2016029570 | ISBN 9780870718656 (paperback)
Subjects: LCSH: Dieterle, Eric—Travel—West (U.S.) | Authors, American—Biography. | Human beings—Effect of environment on. | Identity(Psychology) | Self realization. | Self-actualization (Psychology) | West (U.S.)—Description and travel. | BISAC: NATURE / Essays.
Classification: LCC PS3604.I2254 Z46 2016 | DDC 818/.603 [B] —dc23
LC record available at https://lccn.loc.gov/2016029570

∞This paper meets the requirements of ANSI/NISO Z39.48-1992 (Permanence of Paper).

© 2016 Eric Dieterle
All rights reserved.
First published in 2016 by Oregon State University Press
Printed in the United States of America

OSU

Oregon State
UNIVERSITY

OSU Press

Oregon State University Press
121 The Valley Library
Corvallis OR 97331-4501
541-737-3166 • fax 541-737-3170
www.osupress.oregonstate.edu

for g

Contents

Acknowledgments

This is a work derived from memory. I have been motivated by a quest for artistry, a respect for the truth, and compassion for all mentioned herein. I acknowledge that some of the text originates from previously published material, and gratefully credit the following publications and publishers: *knotgrass*, Sage Publications (*Organization & Environment*), *isotope*, *Watershed* (at Brown University); and *ISLE*, Volume 9.2, Summer 2002, pp. 225–230, "Wasteland or Sanctuary? Post-Apocalyptic Life in a Nuclear Landscape," Oxford University Press. Thanks to those faculty and staff who guided me at Columbia Basin College, Washington State University, Iowa State University, College of the Canyons, Truckee Meadows Community College, and Northern Arizona University; to Roger Kendall for his copyediting acumen; and to Paul Zarzyski for his unvarnished review and support. And to g and m: This book is possible due to to your love and support.

In the Dust below Horse Heaven Hills

STACKED BAGS OF ROCK SALT loomed high in a dim, cavernous room, where the stale smell of diesel exhaust from hulking delivery trucks lingered long after they were parked for the day. I retreated there when I could, to my quiet place, a bunker in the shadows. The comforting crunch and crinkle of the double-layered paper bags measured my movements in steady, careful increments.

My family lived in the back rooms of a soft water supply store in Sunnyside, a little town in Washington State that would be easy for anyone envisioning pine trees, mountains, or ocean to over-look. It was the fourth or fifth home I had been displaced to by the time I was four. From the front office, a showroom window opened to a landscape of railroad tracks and storage buildings across Industrial Avenue. The street led in one direction to a poul-try processing plant, and in the other toward the middle of town.

Descending from the sanctuary of the blue and white bags, I could slip outside and wander along a patch of unkempt grass between home and a neighboring house. Sometimes, the children who came and went from there—brown skinned, black haired—played in the grass, too, and once, as they did so, an alluring smell of fresh-cooked food filled the warm afternoon like sunshine. They invited me to follow them, and I did, entering the house to the sounds of Spanish and the intoxicating promise of home-made flour tortillas being drawn from the oven. Offered one of the warm, soft shells by the matriarch of the household—mother or grandmother, I didn't know—I savored the flavor and aroma.

But before I finished the mysterious treat, hesitation gripped me. Maybe I wasn't supposed to be there. I had drifted to the place, accepted the invitation, without any dialogue in my mind. Now rang the voice of my grandmother, telling me not to speak to those people, not even to breathe around them, and I could see my mother's face, disappointed with my choice. And I imagined the presence of my father; the idea filled me with fear and longing.

I left that strange kitchen with a love for a new taste and many questions about what I had done. Whose voice rose above the rest to send me into that new place? Not the same voice that brought me back home. Not the one that stayed silent against my father's unfathomable moods, or that fell empty at the feet of my mother's distractions. Not the one that clenched and choked when the day finally came, for it felt as if it had been coming, when they hurled their anger at one another one final time before the door slammed for good. Not the voice that meekly offered "OK" at the prospect of another man taking my father's place.

Time and distance tatter chronology, leaving patchwork impressions of places and the person I tried to be in each of them. There is little oral history of this time from my life, no thread of family stories to hold together images or remnants of feelings. But I do remember that by around the age of five, I felt I needed to hide who I was on the inside, and who I was on the outside depended wholly on where I was and whom I was with. I did not know how to tell the truth about myself, or even that the truth was a lesson I would ever need to learn.

Walking straight to my grandparents' apartment from kindergarten, on a road winding up steep Harrison Heights Hill, emerged one day as a natural alternative to walking home. My desire to be in that place simply guided me there. I had learned about the town beyond my home by walking through it—ordered to do so by my mother, despite my tearful protests and anxiety about the unknown. Sunnyside unveiled itself as a place of narrow sidewalks and shop-front windows, where workers I heard called migrants mixed among the small population of the agricultural town. I held my breath as I passed them while navigating those streets five days a week—sometimes alone, sometimes with a few other kids from the neighborhood—and yes, and I do remember hearing something about it years later from my mother: that I seemed happy and confident to make that trek.

And on this day, confident enough to choose my grandmother's kitchen.

I stood there often enough to regard it as a natural condition: leaning against a small metal tabletop painted white with red trim, sturdy on chrome legs, as she spent hours preparing coffee cake or kifli from scratch. She pulled flour from sacks that could be made into dresses and narrated each step in a thick German accent. Her wavy red hair and gold-capped teeth manifested the intensity of all she said and did, including the life lessons layered upon me as she rolled and built delicate flour crusts: Don't put your arm out a car window because a man once had his cut off by a car coming the other way. Don't step on the rails at any crossings in town because they will electrocute you. Don't cross that bridge over the canal on the way to the park because it will collapse and you will die.

I listened as I watched and waited for my next delicious opportunity, and this is what the small apartment meant to me: coffee cake, sausage and cheese, shot glasses of powerful homemade wine—breakfast "eye openers" my grandfather called them—and main dishes and desserts inspired by years of farm living in North Dakota and generations of ethnic heritage brought over on a boat at the turn of the twentieth century.

Eventually on that day of wandering, my grandfather called my mother on the phone, and with a grin asked, "Guess who we have here with us?" I was smiling, too, but it didn't last. My mother reacted with fury. I had seen that force before and would experience it again, and only after many years, through the drip, drip,

drip of exposition and confession, would I learn enough to piece together why.

My great-grandparents, if the written stories from a reunion I did not attend are reliable, had homesteaded after arriving in New York from Bessarabia in 1902. The farm did well, and when my grandfather married my grandmother, they had more than most. Forty years later, living in that small apartment, they still had more than most, although they lived as misers, reusing aluminum foil and paper napkins, which my grandmother showed me how to fold and fold again, so they might last for days. We used honey and butter from packets hoarded after occasional visits to KFC, and after each trip to the grocery store we practiced the ritual of comparing the price of each item to the receipt and would return to the store for even a few pennies. Yet as a child, I watched them open envelopes with checks received from North Dakota address-es—payments from loans they had made to fellow farmers over the years. Frequently their chopped-up English segued seamlessly into German as they spoke, especially when old friends visited. I didn't ask about who they were or what any of the German meant. Instead I spent my time enjoying my grandmother's sublime cook-ing or rode along on the wooden cart my grandfather used to col-lect the trash in his job as apartment building superintendent.

But those were carefree moments enjoyed in fragile times. What action, what comment would silence the kitchen prattling and bring the cataclysm? Like a dark storm looming over the northern plains, roiling with the tension of rising voices, the fight would rise up and lash the landscape. My body shrank and my mind crawled into its own safe space when popped veins and flying spittle erupt-ed amidst guttural skeins of shouted German, a punishing tongue when used as a weapon. My grandmother muttering "Schwein Hund" at my grandfather's back usually signaled the end. Those were the quietest moments, when I could hear my clothes scruff across the carpet as I shifted and waited to be sure.

All I remember about moving to the Tri-Cities is riding in a car and watching the landscape turn to dusty brown. Someone was trying to explain to me about where I was going, but I was already a jaded audience. My family—now a stepfather, two younger sisters, my mother, and me—was moving nearly two hours' drive from Yakima. I'd lived in Yakima twice, long enough to watch a few stalks of corn grow in a small garden out back of a rented house and to celebrate one birthday. Even fifty years later, I can still feel the visceral panic of my first day at a new school and the episode that ruined my attitude toward math for life, as a teacher handed me worksheets that might as well have been written in hieroglyphics. I wished so profoundly to disappear, to escape from the indecipherable problems, from the unfamiliar teacher, from the faces of children I did not know and did not want to know.

So I entered this new place, which itself seemed to exist in isolation, and I watched the miles unfold through eyes that regarded the landscape with more suspicion than wonderment, and with a heart in which fear leaned heavily into the excitement of exploration.

Our small house sat in a working-class neighborhood in a town called Kennewick. Some people also called the place the Tri-Cities, and I reasoned that the nearby towns of Pasco and Richland had something to do with that. Our streets were a labyrinth of asphalt laid over—according to a neighbor—a graveyard of vineyards that stretched over the hilly south end of town. Just a few houses down and across a busier street than our own, an irrigation canal cut through an undeveloped swath of scabland, and I found myself attracted to the water, where I built bridges and dams out of the rocks and litter all around. A triple tower of concrete irrigation standpipes stood in our backyard, and none of us ever fully grasped their purpose or placement. We just understood that water from a hose could run endlessly from this source at nearly no cost to our money-starved household, allowing us to have a lawn where nature intended dust. And from that same source sprang a garden. I learned from trenching, weeding, and watering that soil was for cultivation, and what I did not know then was that my fascination with watching the dirt darken with moisture spoke of connections to family, to the river, and to the landscape itself.

My grandparents' apartment was now fifty miles northwest. Only a few minutes away from there, in a parallel universe, my stepfather's parents lived on a small farm. Down home people from rural Idaho, who had raised their three sons next to the Teton River, they lived a true farm life, gathering eggs each day from the henhouse, slopping the few hogs they owned, cultivating a patch of corn, milking the cows that wandered their twelve-acre pasture.

We traveled to the farm most weekends, sometimes also spending an hour at the apartment. The road became familiar and I marked the time not by a watch, but by watching out the car window. Often draped with the silvery sheen of heat mirages, Highway 12 ventured along the base of the Horse Heaven Hills and in sight of the shallow Yakima River, nudging ever more northward on its way to Sunnyside.

As we headed out from Kennewick, desolation spread across a dusty, wan canvas. The dull aqua of sagebrush dotted parched, tan earth. Wheat fields blanketed the tops of the hills, but they were above and out of sight; only brown, barren hillsides, notched from erosion and occasional runoff, filled the view from the window. The first signs of agriculture told me we were more than halfway. Long aluminum sprinkler pipes on wheels patrolled circle farms, arcing sprays of water over fields of potatoes, and asparagus pushed up like pins from the ground. Then for a few miles, angular arrays of poles and cables leaned over fields of hops. After that, if the season were right, the pungent breeze of mint would mark the final stretch.

Finally, the farm, about a half-mile down a gravel road. Hay fields sloped down to the one-story house, and from there a rutted dirt road ran farther downhill to a shed for milking, a henhouse, and a small pigpen. I climbed bales of hay and raided a bin of dried corncobs, which became missiles or footballs, depending on my mood, and I learned how to prime a pump and draw water by raising and lowering the metal handle at an even pace and pressure. I was told not to drink but the miracle was enough—move the handle up and down with just the right force, and listen as gasps of air gave way to water appearing from nowhere.

At meals, a cast of characters gathered at a big table set up in the living room. Grandpa, hard of hearing, shouted his sentences over a blaring television and lumbered to his place with a cane in each hand. "Maw!" he'd yell, signaling a request. Grandma, decades of determination furrowed into her farm-weathered face, hurried from kitchen to table with pot and dish and platter. Another whom we called "grandma," who lived alone in a tiny house in town and called her friends sister and brother, would fuss and wonder if we would ever settle down. Uncle Fred, the ancient one whose true relation to the family—if there was any—I never understood, appeared from his room as mysteriously as the water from the well but was even more difficult to fathom. He rarely spoke. So he startled me when once I was seated next to him and he leaned toward me. "At night when you're asleep," he said, motioning to indicate the farmhouse, "spiders crawl into your mouth."

Rudolph, another mysterious live-in, would stride into the room wearing spurs and chaps, muttering something about his day on the ranch. He talked more than any of us, but usually to himself or to someone across from him who was invisible to the rest of us. Grandma's surveillance of the mailbox out by the road sometimes turned up catalog orders for expensive saddles or other cowboy accoutrements. Rudolph didn't seem to notice that they never arrived.

We gathered to sprawling spreads of meat, potatoes, and vegetables, with thick, fresh milk extracted from beneath a three-inch layer of cream in a gallon jar. After dinner, Grandpa leaned over with his plate, leaving it on the floor for King, the family dog, to lick clean.

I could barely eat. The rawness of the food, the people, the place unnerved me. Had the dog cleaned the fork I was about to put in my mouth? Did that glass of milk not just come from a jar that came from a pail that came from under Bossy's udder? I called these people "grandpa" and "grandma" and "uncle," but I did not feel it. I sat there but I did not belong. Because miles away at the apartment, clean and ordered, I would be reminded to sit straight and sit still, keep quiet, eat from shiny plates with immaculate silverware, and stop wiping my face on my sleeve—only those dirty, brown children do such things—but use the tiniest remaining clean corner of my napkin.

Until the freeway came, only that same two-lane stretch of asphalt that had brought us to Sunnyside connected southeastern Washington State to the west. After Sunnyside, the highway edged northwest past Toppenish and Wapato, until it reached Yakima. There highway merged into freeway, then pointed north as it climbed over the dry, empty Umptanum Ridge. At Ellensburg it opened to a spectacular vista, the expansive, fertile Kittitas Valley in the shadows of the Wenatchee Mountains. As green assumed ascendancy and pine trees gobbled up the sky, the road bent northwest to begin the long climb to Snoqualmie Pass. From the summit, it would plummet and twist like a bobsled run with the finish line at Seattle. For most of the winter, a bobsled run would have been safer. Snow falls in the Cascade Mountains by the foot. On both sides of the pass, the road widens at several points so drivers can chain up their tires and try to cross.

Sometimes the pass closes. Sometimes avalanches bury it. Snow piles ten feet or higher on the shoulders of the road in walls built by persistent snowplows.

About 220 miles from the Tri-Cities to Seattle. A four-hour drive in good weather. A dramatic change in landscape. It became a familiar and frightening stretch of road, linking me to the indecipherable life of my intermittently present father, who by making Seattle his home ultimately fenced it off from ever being mine.

Whenever my father followed through on his stated plans about his monthly visitation, he would arrive, almost always late, to pick up my sister and me from our Kennewick home. Often we went with him only as far as Sunnyside and the apartment. The prospect filled me with dread. He drove with anger, speeding, passing around corners and up hills, risking it all to fling us around the next car, and the next one. He yelled and cursed as if in heated conflict with every one of them, and I had only one thought: I will die this way. The landscape and the harrowing reality in the car receded as I took shelter within myself.

But he was my father. When he laughed, he laughed freely, crooked teeth and all, a glint of untarnished happiness in his blue eyes. He spoke with deep pride about the family name and looked ahead, as he said again and again, to a better life for me and my sister than he'd had for himself. He held promise in a wallet full of more money than I ever saw at home.

I did not know how to be with him. Because a word, a movement—a leaf twitching on a branch in the breeze, for all I knew— was enough to send him to the far edges of a temper that swelled within me as it flew from him, pressing tears to my eyes that I could not let fall. But there was something else. To my child's mind, the man I knew as father swerved into someone I did not know, and I could not keep up. Was he really a special agent for the FBI or just pretending for my sake? Did the Air Force whisper about some dark potential he possessed, or was it just a story? Some reflex caused me to look away when he said these things, and I wished he would not say them.

Yet there was a time before he left our home—I heard a noise outside early one morning and stood on a chair to look out my high bedroom window. I saw a panel truck next door and people loading something in the back. Later that morning, I heard talk at breakfast that a boat motor had been stolen from the neighbors. I said I had seen it happen. What I remember next is driving slowly through downtown with my father, trying to find the truck. We were working with the police. Or he was the police. Someone kept asking, "Is it that one? Is it that one?" while pointing to different vehicles, and finally I said, "That one," but I was misunderstood. They checked the wrong one and said nothing was there. I felt powerless to protest, "No, not that one. That other one." And I felt shame at my story unraveling. Yet he believed me. Our worlds had intersected, and we spent part of a morning in a place no one else could see or understand.

My mother says it never happened. Whether it did or didn't, my questions began to arise about who my father was, and who I was when I was with him, and how negotiable identity could be in a world that didn't seem to be the right place for either of us.

The first gun may have been the nickel-plated .357. He wore it in a shoulder holster, under a sport coat jacket. I wasn't afraid of it at first, not knowing of its potential as a weapon or as an extension of self. The silver fascinated me. Its long angles were beautiful, the weight impressive. There would be more, but this was the first one I saw and held, and ultimately, fired, the ringing in my ears a lingering reminder of its explosive power.

Sometimes he would introduce us, my sister and me, to a woman. I lost track of who was a friend and who was . . . more? Was he married to one of them? Once we stopped at the home of a wrinkled blonde with a raspy voice. She talked about being a country and western singer, which I didn't believe until she brought out a promotional photo from her younger days. She made me squirm under her leering, knowing stares, an aura of cigarette smoke hovering around her beehive hairdo. Yet upon leaving her place I owned my first guitar, a gift from her. It turned out to be the only instrument I ever learned to play.

He was my father.

The Cascades divided my life as clearly as they divided the geography of the state. When my father took us all the way back to Seattle, that road, treacherous as it was, opened a portal to being someplace else and someone else. Once safely there, I welcomed escape from the desert and a place no one seemed to have heard of. My father's visits were a passage to a life of restaurants and gifts, games and concerts and downtown lights, the smell of ocean in the air. I experienced the cult of fish tossing at Pike Place Market, spent afternoons at uncrowded Alki Beach, looked out at Puget Sound and the urban skyline from a moving car on the Alaska Way Viaduct and felt the comfortable rumble of the grating on the Spokane Street drawbridge.

As a young boy, I did not know in any worldly way about guns or other women, or about the slow torment of family secrets. But I understood desperation and the bony clutch of fear constricting my throat. And worse, the anticipation of what strange or temper-fueled event might come next, like a heavy blanket weighing on my head, my heart racing to catch itself in thinning air. Like the bitter taste of salt lingering in my dry mouth.

My mother's parents hauled their travel trailer across forty-eight states. They brought it to Kennewick a couple of times, and I reveled in the magic of their appearance from the world beyond. When they invited me into their tiny trailer, parked in our driveway, I tingled at the notion of stepping into another world. The smell of freshly brewed Sanka stirred a sense of warm comfort. I can still smell the toast cooked on a contraption that looked like a metal tee-pee over their gas stove. One year, my great-grandparents accompanied them, bringing their own trailer and tales of travel, sharing with me a bowl of snapping turtle soup from their most recent foray into Minnesota.

But after what seemed only a short visit, my grandparents would disappear into the next journey. I was lucky to see them once a year, or two, or three. And even luckier when I could see them at their home in Indiana. My first experience of landscape on a grand scale came during my second cross-country train trip when I was in grade school. (The first, when I was much younger, had left only thematic imprints: the imposing engines, smelling of diesel, their gentle rumble rising as they throttled up.) I virtually lived in a dome car, absorbing the off-road beauty of Glacier National Park, thrilling to long tunnels through the Rockies, high trestles across rivers, and herds of antelope on the open plains. The constant movement and rhythmic rocking embraced me. My mother, sisters, and I subsisted on boxes of Chicken in a Biskit and occasional meals in the dining car over three and a half days of mile-consuming adventure.

The experience was not just transportation; it was transport to a world from which I came but that I barely knew. Our destination, a cottage owned by my great-grandparents at Big Lake, lay just outside Columbia City.

Probably I could sense from my mother that this was home. I had been born in nearby Huntington, in the same hospital on the banks of the Wabash in which she had been born. But somehow, when I was younger than two, the Hoosier girl ended up in Washington. I had already lived in Ft. Wayne, Spokane, Yakima, and Sunnyside, and I have to believe there's a reason that the smells of warm toast smeared with apple butter, the barefoot trips to the outhouse bathroom, the thunderheads rising over the lake all felt so right.

Big Lake encompassed a world of hot, humid days, fishing for bluegill with a cane pole or trolling for something bigger in my great-grandfather's boat. I would awaken in the cottage each morning, pull on a pair of swim trunks, and walk down to the lake for a morning swim. I'd hold my breath for a trip under the surface to greet the curious fish that loitered by a small wooden boat dock. At night, I'd marvel at ferocious thunderstorms, the boom from one hissing bolt of lightning rattling the chairs on the kitchen floor, or go outside and play among the lightning bugs. They intrigued me so deeply that I captured a dozen or so in a jar with the sincere intent of taking them back to Kennewick, where I planned to release them to create my own lightning bug population. Nearly all of them survived the train trip home, and with a heart full of hope I set them free under a white birch in our front yard. But I never saw them again, never saw their lights in the dry desert nights.

My attempt to blend separate worlds had failed. At Big Lake, I was the barefoot midwestern boy. At the farm of my stepdad's parents, I was left to my imagination. At the apartment I experienced alternating joy and fear between sweet treats and bitter arguments. In Seattle, I felt at home in my heart but increasingly uneasy with the person who took me there. I belonged everywhere and nowhere. In each place I could act out a separate and distinct me, while no one was allowed to know who lay within. And from each place, I always returned to the desert. There, under the wide, blue sky, I would engage in the long struggle to discover who I really was.

River of Wind

"LET'S GO FOR A DRIVE."

These words from one of my parents incited a fight between me and my sisters about who would get a window seat. The family car, a hulking, white Pontiac Catalina, could have held five kids in the back but a window meant status, or maybe revenge for the most recent sibling slight. I blamed the green interior for my car sickness, and a window may have brought some respite, but I would not admit that weakness in making a claim against younger sisters, one by three years, one by six.

Status aside, I wanted to see, as if the next drive would bring something different. I can't say my young heart yet understood despair. Or the oppression of sameness. But my eyes revealed a truth of sage and more sage, no end to it beyond the edges of town, infiltrating every vacant lot, so common that I didn't merely see it—I understood it as the binding that held the world together.

Knowing that God created the world, I wondered if he'd gotten tired by the time this part had come along. The words I heard most often—basin, plateau, basalt—led to the same definition: dull, flat, empty. (And later, I learned the more sophisticated scablands and sagebrush-steppe, which inevitably yielded to the expletive Dry Shitties or ironic Three Jewels.)

In this land I learned my first lessons about hundred-degree heat and the searing consequence of skin burned red. My parents taught us that shadows were places for rattlesnakes and black widow spiders. They called out the warnings again and again on family outings: don't sit on a rock and dangle your legs over an outcrop or an opening in the soil below; don't poke around near the base of a large sage. Look up in enclosed spaces and check around. Listen. Watch your step. Watch your reach.

The inescapable sky reflected sunlight like a mirror. Waves of heat radiated up from the ground or bled into the air from brick and concrete. An arid, unseen force banished rain, or even the hope of it.

Across the emptiness roamed a restless apparition. Wind, the empty residue of hope—no clouds, no rain, just wind. As inescapable as if it had always been present, as if in the beginning there was wind. With the awareness of God it found every place, every moment, and entered with the reminder of its existence. A breeze might flutter the gray-green leaves at the tops of gnarled cottonwoods or coax ripples to rise on the Columbia River's surface, turning a placid mirror into frosted glass. Sometimes the ghost would take shape as a wisp of cloud, twisting in diaphanous silence across the cobalt blue sky. Occasionally, as if taking its own breath for a brief moment, the wind would cease and the world stopped and waited, unsure of how to proceed in the calm.

More often, the moment portended a blustering, eye-squinting, hair-thrashing blow that might last ten minutes or ten days. Those insistent storms rose within me in gusts of nervous anticipation. At night, I'd lie in my bed unsheltered from the howls as great rushes of momentum that had gathered over the desert hurled themselves into the house, shaking it with menace. Transformed by fear, the wind conjured images that a dam had broken, the water from behind it rushing in to engulf the world and me with it. Wind cut the swirling boundary between consciousness and sleep, which I feared most of all because blown deep into that dark land, I might never return.

Daytime brought no escape or respite. The wind wore on me the way it wore on the landscape. The air carried the grit of irritation, anger rose as whitecaps roiled across the Columbia, frustration built as high branches bent until, even when peace finally came, they were hunched in the prevailing direction of the wind.

If the wind blew for enough days, the earth itself would rise up to join it. Flying sand colored the air so brown, people used headlights to drive through town during the day. Gusts stung our faces with billions of sharp granules. Waves of sand hurled against concrete buildings, sounding like the simmer of a beach exposed by a pulsing ocean. We hunched and stumbled, shielding our faces and eyes when struggling to move outside, entering a dwelling with a sandy gust and a blessing for having reached sanctuary. The end of such a storm constituted an otherworldly experience. Warily, people ventured into the eerie glow of dusk as the wind finally died, dust still thick in the air, diffusing light from the horizon. Fences, filters of the moveable landscape, leaned under a plaster cast of litter and tumbleweeds. The silence brought its own uneasiness. My numbed mind refused to let go of a world that had been in perpetual motion.

I don't know how that world, fifty miles from my earliest memories of landscape, could be so different. Maybe my awareness awakened and spread out along the open plateau, experiencing its details with more intensity and understanding. This was the beginning of the idea of home—same place, same family, same school. And in a town of fourteen thousand, the same streets, and stores, and faces. Time and repetition allowed the elements of place to populate my growing consciousness. There, on the interior, was where change took root. Anchored in the desert, I could begin to learn more about me. I would have a stern and steady guide.

I'd been to church before. In Sunnyside, church had been an uncomfortable place to sit quietly after a morning of light play with nicely dressed kids and a few strains of "Jesus loves me, yes I know." But the desert sparked a flame in my mother's heart. Sundays became ritual, with the only variable being a choice between early service or late, with Sunday School between. Some familiarity eased the transition. Red brick and stained glass with sharp, arched roofs containing a vaulted worship room linked with dark brown wooden pews. Inside, organ music poured over the thick syrup of funerary liturgy pronounced by somber, stiff-backed men and women with German surnames and accents like those of my German grandparents. Together we sat and stood to ancient choreography: the pious dance of the Lutheran Church, Missouri Synod. Stand, sit, sing, speak, listen, confess, pray. Slow, laboring hymns, the somber drone of the Nicene Creed, prayers as endless as the plateau. Even within that human-built godly space in an enclave of old-growth maples, the message fit the landscape. Back to basics, the pastor preached. Stick to the Gospel. Just straight-ahead, old-fashioned, take-it-or-leave-it religion. God said what He had to say.

I gulped that message as if I were granted permission for the clear, cold water from the farm pump. But the meaning, on its way in, underwent a twist. I was shown drawings of Jesus surrounded by little children and told that all of us, even the grownups, should approach him as children. Ah, but I was not one of them. Jesus and I had a personal relationship—really personal—and the joke was on everyone else. And I was a little envious. He turned water into wine? Bread into fishes? And if we believe, we can move mountains? It would only be a matter of time, I reasoned, until I could perform such miracles. Then the world would know of me and my potential. "When?" became my central question, so I said the words and sang the songs, and I waited. I confessed my sins, some clearer to me than others, and anticipated the stage of the structured service that told me we were nearly done. If I daydreamed past it, the smells floating up from the basement—brewing coffee and fresh pastries—snapped me to attention. Lutherans liked their food.

What awaited me, besides release, might be just a day at home—watching some football and playing in the yard—or a trip north for a visit, or sometimes, that Sunday drive. Whether those afternoons were actually open-ended or my parents knew of our destination, I welcomed them with anticipation because we were likely to end up at a river. By the time my family moved to within a couple of miles of its banks, the Columbia barely resembled its original self—a fact unknown to me as a child, although the well-ordered levees hinted of intervention. The Columbia is a mile wide as it courses along and through the Tri-Cities. The confluence of the Snake and Columbia lies just upstream, and the Yakima adds shallow, choppy waters ten miles downstream, their joining hidden from the highway but known to me on all those trips to Sunnyside as a curved swath of green in the midst of nothing.

The Columbia could be crossed by the Blue Bridge or the Old Bridge, as we knew them, one a four-lane gentle arc high above the water and the other a narrow, nerve-wracking test of driver discipline and faith. (One day, I would face it as the final gauntlet of driver education class.) But a drive over either bridge brought a long view of the wide, blue swath of water.

Our family drive might be to a park or a dam, and I was always trying to untangle the geography in my mind. The Columbia flowed west from town to the ocean after bending east, then back around. Driving south twenty-five miles would take us to McNary Dam and the border with Oregon. Yet we'd also cross the river going north, then turn east to reach the Snake. This was our most frequent day trip, taking us through downtrodden east Pasco, then along fields of wheat and potatoes to Ice Harbor Dam. The towers of the dam's locks resembled the crenelated chess piece symbol of the Army Corps of Engineers, whose signage welcomed us and whose dioramas and brochures explained what we were viewing and why it was there.

We'd park in the visitor's lot and walk up to the walls of the lock, peering over the edge to check the water level. I marveled at the dam's thickness and strength yet discovered a weakness of my own. If the water in the lock were low, it drew me with some unnamed, frightening force. "Come to me," I could almost hear it whisper, and my head swooned as my legs prepared to comply. The urge, the compulsion arising from within—that was the really confusing part. Why did I want to jump? I learned to grip the cold concrete with the edges of my fingers to ground myself, and over time and many visits I also learned that some days were more difficult than others, and that if the strange desire swept over me from the moment I left the car, it was easier not to approach the locks at all.

Some days we'd spend more time at the dam; others, we'd walk along the riprap shoreline. I'd throw rocks into the water or search for driftwood. On a sweltering afternoon, which was most, we might skip the dam altogether and go straight to Levey Landing, a park, by my estimation, but a fine example of public recreation, according to the corps. From the potential of the untamed river, they proclaimed, opportunities were created by lazy stretches of open water, inviting water skiers and leisure boaters, and bringing families on picnics to formerly rough, uninviting shores. There were such examples up and down the rivers, and we visited many of them: Fishhook and Sacawajea, also on the Snake, or Two Rivers on the Columbia.

But the parks were mere window dressing for the real purpose of the river. At 1,243 miles long, according to the literature, the Columbia fell twice as fast as the Mississippi, giving it huge hydroelectric potential, much of it put to good use by eleven dams. Its waters irrigated thousands of farms and orchards, and the lawns and trees I grew up assuming had always been there. Even the part of the river I knew best, where barges loaded with wheat ploughed a wake at the insistent urging of tugboats, was called by another name: Lake Wallula, according to a corps map.

Beneath the water, thousands of salmon and steelhead navigated the river on spawning runs. Each day, the newspaper published the official "fish count." At dams on the Columbia and Snake Rivers, employees of the Army Corps of Engineers sat at the window of a concrete office and counted the number and type of fish that passed over one of the many dams on the river. The fish were herded through a fish ladder—an ascending concrete trough with evenly spaced dividers meant to simulate the rapids the salmon would have encountered had the dam not been there. At the top of the ladder, they swam through a narrow channel over a white-painted board on their way to the other side of the dam. As various types of fish crossed the board, a worker tabulated them. When we visited Ice Harbor, we peered into the water to see the fish ourselves. It never struck me then how perverse a scene had been created—fish attempting to follow their natural instincts through a concrete contraption while people gathered to watch, leaning over the monolithic blocks of gray with their backs turned to the very river that the fish were meant to navigate in the first place.

Sometimes we fished as a family, but not for salmon. We lacked a boat and the proper equipment. One of us might be lucky enough to hook a bottom-dwelling catfish—good to eat but hard to clean, with sharp bones protruding from its misshapen head—but more likely our catch would be a scaly carp or a bony whitefish, both regarded as inedible, or the hideous sucker with bloated lips of gristle and a sloping head. I despised that fish, with its looks of a dullard, and I was taught that suckers were not to be thrown back, but rather tossed onto the shore to suffocate in the heat the way a trash fish deserved. I threw rocks at their heads or slit open their bellies to hasten death. After all, they sucked mud from the bottom of the river to extract their food. Even their dull yellow underside appeared unclean.

It would be decades before I learned that the sucker I had so despised and heaved ashore in frustration had a significance that rivaled the salmon's. Historically, Indians along the Columbia regarded the sucker as a food fish. They would catch it in great numbers before the annual salmon run. When cooked, the bones of its skull fell into separate pieces and storytellers would spin tales about the origins of each piece, based on its appearance. I've since thought of all the sucker skulls I left on the shoreline and all the tales they could have spawned, had I known.

But even as a sucker-chucking, thoughtless child, the river's whispers slipped through my blindness for compassion and found me in mysterious ways. In my first experience of the Potholes, where my stepdad took me to reap a stringer-full of hatchery trout on opening day, I fished from tiny lakes, the artifacts left behind on the plateau when ancient forces of fire and ice shifted the great river's course. Grey hexagonal columns of basalt walled off shorelines here and there, preserving the story, if I would listen, and watching over the ghosts of the river's deep past.

In town, from the vista along Canal Drive, I gazed at the river-lake, wide and flat, and followed the blue that extended into opposite horizons. From there, I could also see the edges of Columbia Park, a two-mile-long corridor of grass, sand, and trees bisected by a remnant of the Old Inland Empire Highway. Most of the shoreline along Columbia Park, as it is on many other stretches of the river, was artificial, made up of jagged rocks placed there before the dams as a flood-control mechanism. Wading was treacherous in the fifty-degree water driven by a swift current, and the sharp rock was unforgiving in a fall. It was easier to squat in about a foot of the chilly water and float out, if you could stand the cold.

We didn't go there to swim—the muddy Snake offered warmer water and gooey muck that swallowed our feet and didn't bite. The park was more often a place for a picnic with a burger and fries, with precocious seagulls swarming us. But the park assumed a new meaning in my life on a late-July day in 1967. My mother took me there to see unlimited hydroplanes. Most of the boats were about twenty-eight feet long and powered by hulking V-12 Rolls Royce engines, a type used in World War II fighter plans.

I could hear them on the river from our backyard. The racing circuit, established in the 1950s—along with the reputation of danger and death that accompanied boats skimming across the water at nearly two hundred miles per hour—included Madison and Evansville, Indiana, and Detroit, Seattle, and San Diego. Now the Tri-Cities, as part of an annual celebration called the Water Follies, became a host.

As my mother and I walked from the car across the rough mix of grass and weeds that covered most of the park, a roar unlike anything I'd ever experienced shook me. As we hurried to the river, I caught my first sight of a hydroplane on the water. *Chrysler Crew*, powered by two auto racing engines running in tandem, bounced and skipped as it threw thousands of gallons of water in an arc behind it—a rooster tail, I would learn it was called.

That moment launched an obsession. The speed, power, and spectacle thrilled me. Of all the brightly colored boats, I fell in love with *My Gypsy*, resplendent yet mysterious in her dark hues of orange wrapped in wispy black. She was beautiful and my allegiance a purely emotional one. When she entered the water, placed there by a massive crane, I stood on a rock at the river's edge to feel as fully as I could the vibration of sound screaming from the polished aircraft engine.

My family was one of thousands on race day that drove in, parked on the shoulder of the road aimed at the river, and set up camp with lawn chairs, beach towels, and umbrellas. Those casual outings did not last long; over time, the Water Follies devolved. During a gathering of forty thousand people in hundred-degree weather over eight hours of intermittent racing, attention inevitably turned away from a forbiddingly frigid river to free-flowing alcohol, copious drugs, and bikini-clad young women. After about ten years, the mini-Woodstock sparked a battle between civil patrons and the faction that wore T-shirts declaring, "If you can't rock 'n' roll, don't fucking come." The decline of that ephemeral civilization paralleled my own changes. As a young boy, shielded from the world by parents and church, I drank sodas and stood mesmerized by the bone-rattling roar. By my early twenties, I had perfected my techniques to smuggle in alcohol past ever more stringent security, and at my pinnacle shared swigs of Crown Royal with a guy who said he was Rockin' Rollen, the rainbow-haired icon of major sporting events who years later swapped out the booze for a John 3:16 placard.

What did not change was the strange innuendo of late afternoon. Tingling in the afterglow of the day's events, I ritually remained by the water as the crowd streamed away. A day of racing left the river snarling, whitecaps and whirlpools scribbling memories of a lost river across the surface in a language unknown to me.

Those waves pulsed at a time when the wider world crept into my awareness, and it was a world of violence. I was introduced to what assassination was with JFK but was more fascinated with the flag-covered coffin drawn by horses than I was frightened by death. With the deaths of Bobby Kennedy and Martin Luther King Jr., I understood death a little more and worried about its finality, and as I listened to the daily body count from Vietnam on the radio each morning, the numbers began to feel ominous.

That the river and death could somehow mingle is probably best explained by the confusion of an immature mind trying to make sense of it all, but it happened. On family outings along the river I often saw hidden places of matted-down grass and weeds littered with beer cans, food wrappers, and a sock, or a shirt, or a pair of panties. Maybe a filthy mattress or broken chair lay nearby. I wondered what happened in these places—after dark, no doubt—and the wondering turned to a dry gulp in my throat after the Manson murders. The newspaper headlines blared about Sharon Tate because she was considered a local girl. In a moment, those mysterious, littered spaces transformed into sites of torture and murder.

Still, I did not fear the river—only the artifacts of human activity and bad intention.

But the river contributed to my loss of innocence on a family outing to The Dalles Dam on the Washington-Oregon border, when I learned for the first time about Celilo Falls. Several pictures hung on the wall of the visitors' center. They showed a wild, frothing river cascading over a gauntlet of rock. I learned that the falls were killed in March 1957, just a little more than a year before I was born, when flooding from the dam drowned them. As I stood there, an awareness percolated through me. I understood loss. Out there somewhere, under the swollen river, lay the true course of the Columbia, out of sight, dark and cold like a sunken ship. The moment felt like death.

That day pushed me past my barrier of engineering dogma. I imagined the river had a soul. My eyes opened with knowledge; I learned about the lie of the fish count and how few salmon truly remained. In 1805, Lewis and Clark described a river surging with salmon. Native Americans had built a culture around the salmon. Those beautiful fish had a certain nobility. Silver and shiny, they represented strength, beauty, challenge—the essence of the original river.

Moving beyond the simple gaze of a child, I grew comfortable speaking to the river, to beseeching it for wisdom, for even though it was swollen and maimed, it had been there for so long and experienced so much in its journey. I turned to the river for peace, calmed by its steady blue current. I looked to the river for meaning, seeking answers to my questions and assurances for my doubts in the ever-changing ripples and swirls.

These feelings rose and fell with moods and life events, but as summer finally relented, acquiescing to the onset of cooler, grayer days, wind and river flowed into one another, and together, through my soul. I spent many hours swept by surges of chilly wind as it whipped riffles across the river, and I allowed both the wind and the river to carry me from the world.

As winter set in, the wind changed its attitude, was still persistent but now also punishing and cold. This message from the north reminded me that Canada lay on the border, a place, it seemed, that should be cold and white in the winter but might as well have been a world away from the lifeless brown plateau. Perhaps the north would send snow, I wished, but much more likely, only the hollow howls of freezing fronts of wind would arrive.

The only other name I knew for wind brought despair to the child who wanted a winter with blankets of white. Chinook. The name of a Native American tribe—a name given to salmon and a pass over the Cascades. But attached to wind, Chinook meant a hot breath of spite blown from the mountains. It was not enough that the westward slopes captured most of the moisture, inches of rain and feet of snow, leaving only a trace or nothing at all for the east. They would also send the Chinook, an assassin sweeping in under cover of darkness to annihilate snow that might have slipped through. In a single night, the Chinook could scour the landscape and leave behind only the dampness of melted snow and the uncomfortable warmth of an unwelcome embrace.

I hated the Chinook for ruining my childhood dreams, for holding up the carcass of my brown, dead home to declare "Here. This is where you live." Yet through the years I learned to understand that honesty is like that; wind may sting or burn or exasperate, but most of all, it tells the truth.

Atoms in the Sand

THE BEGUILING SCENT OF DAMP SAGE at once allures and offends. Under a flat, gray fall sky, the familiar paradox filled my nostrils as I stepped out of the family station wagon for an afternoon of hunting with my stepdad. He carried a long-barreled 12-gauge shotgun and I carried only hope that on this day my meanderings among the sage would stir up a ring-necked pheasant. Brown wild grasses lay limply on the sandy soil, their season having passed, and each step on them released even more pungency into the crisp air.

We were at a place known as Ringold, at the end of a gravel road on a bluff overlooking the Columbia. At least as far as we dared travel on the road, for the unstable ground in that area often slid away from above and below, opening a gaping crevice in the road or burying it in a light brown, grainy flow.

I welcomed yet another view of the river, shallower and a little rougher looking from that juncture, but felt my usual unease when I gazed across the water to what lay beyond. Gray concrete domes and steam towers. Thick, flat-roofed structures that were more bunker than building. Hanford. Even from the distant, wind-blown bluff, the eeriness enveloped me, as odd and difficult to fathom as the smell of the sage. I looked over a cemetery unlike any other. Death had been crafted there—some of it unleashed, some of it awaiting release—and death lurked in the soil. What resonated in my heart was the emptiness, a void that reached across the river.

Hanford, I knew, was the site where bomb-grade plutonium had been produced. Was it still? I'd heard adults claim Hanford was a target—a highlight on the Soviet map of places to take out first if a nuclear war were launched. The gates were guarded by men with machine guns, I was told, and they were but a visible front for the ninjas who slipped in and out of the shadows in their secret vigilance.

I had never been there or even approached the gates and did not know exactly how the complex of reactors, processing plants, and other mysterious buildings were organized. Only that they were out there, scattered across a barren forbidden zone. My stepdad told me about what he had seen. As an office machine repairman, he was granted temporary access through the security gates. I did not understand or appreciate what he perceived in the intricate metal guts of typewriters and photocopiers, but I was impressed that he was allowed inside Hanford to do his work. Dads of other kids I knew worked there every day. These kids lived in nicer houses. Something about their experience of everyday life was different. They belonged in the Tri-Cities in a way that I did not.

The idea of not belonging stirred awake in new and discomfiting ways during my middle school years. My sisters and I switched to a parochial school so that Sunday's lessons could become daily ones. In tiny classes, compared with my public school experience, I sat next to the children of dentists, scientists, and engineers. Not every parent worked at Hanford and not every family had money, but I began to see that most had more than we did. I realized what I had not noticed in church—the clothes, the cars, the air of possession and entitlement. I learned more about my religion and that faith amounted to what I said on the outside and feared on the inside.

Trying to fit in, I weaved my trips to Seattle and the rambling, unverifiable narrative of my father into stories to define me: a street fighter (trained by him), a descendant of stable keepers for Romanian royalty, a privileged member of Seattle society. But I could not fend off the accumulation of daily experience. Bullies and the tyranny of peers troubled me with the reality that I couldn't throw a softball as far as half the girls in my class, and I looked malnourished in my hand-me-down, high-water jeans. An unfortunate school photo taught me I had oily hair and that I shouldn't laugh unguardedly, or even smile, with my crooked teeth. As part of a class exercise in self-awareness, we each secretly wrote a one-word description of our classmates; the teacher compiled them and handed them out. Two words appeared on my list: smart and weird.

I could see reminders of my home's heritage all around me: Atomic Lanes bowling alley. The Atomic Cup trophy for the winner of the hydroplane races. Symbols of atoms and clever plays on words at small businesses and in ads. Even the Tri-Cities themselves, referred to as a unit out of a Chamber of Commerce desire for relevance, were three separate entities drawn together by forces of economic attraction and repelled through class differences. Kennewick felt most comfortable to me, not just as home, but as a collection of neighborhoods more or less like mine. Across the river, Pasco, the smallest of the three but with a large minority population, lay on the southern edge of expansive circle farms of potatoes and wheat. Nine miles west, on the Kennewick side of the river, sat Richland, the nucleus.

My family didn't go there often—we could live our lives well enough between Kennewick and Pasco—but each trip drove home that we had entered a place different from our own. Manicured neighborhoods of military-style housing sent the message that engineers, lab technicians, and managers lived there, people with deep ties to Hanford who were rewarded by the flow of government money. Even the high school imposed itself as a force: the Bombers, a sports powerhouse. Their logo, on football helmets and the banner in their gym, was a mushroom cloud, and their cheerleaders would plant a green and gold replica of a bomb at center court before basketball games.

In the visitor's center of a Department of Energy building in Richland—another venue on our family's free-time itinerary—photos and posters told a story of development in the desert in the style of the Army Corps of Engineers. When the US military launched the Manhattan Project during World War II, planners searched for isolated spaces. Isolated for secrecy. Isolated so that an accident would not destroy civilized territory. Hanford was an ideal place. Blissful monotony lay in that flat, brown, sun-baked land of dry coulees and barren bluffs, with the Rattlesnake Mountains looming to the west. By 1939, the island of empti-ness had attracted only enough interest for a small railroad town and a few struggling farms. But the great river that had always been there now showed more promise, with electricity from Grand Coulee Dam in copious supply, and the cold, swift waters them-selves would play a part—eventually, millions of gallons surged through as many as eight nuclear reactors, heated to two hundred degrees before being dumped back into the river.

Under the atomic imperative of World War II, the small town of Hanford was "disappeared" and in its place Hanford the super-secret government project emerged. To build an atomic bomb re-quired plutonium, only a pinch of which would require processing on a huge scale. Beginning in 1942, an army of construction work-ers and scientists faced the isolation and incessant dust storms of Hanford, separating themselves from civilization for the sake of saving it. The work didn't end after Fat Man obliterated Nagasaki. Hanford processed plutonium for multitudes of nuclear weapons. Eager for some sort of distinction, I adopted Hanford as a point of pride when I was on the other side of the Cascades. There was little hope that anyone knew of the Tri-Cities. People in Seattle marveled at my embellished descriptions of desert-bound life. At least a mention of Hanford elicited an occasional, "Oh, I've heard of that." In those moments, I was reminded how the state in which I lived aroused wide admiration for its endless western horizon, ascendant mountains, and evergreen trees. Yet I lived in its little-known wasteland. So I told the familiar jokes to the west-siders: We could get warm water out of the cold side of the tap. We didn't have to cook our fish—they were already done when we caught them. We didn't have to use night-lights—we glowed in the dark.

I also came to appreciate what the military had recognized: the ease of concealment in the midst of such exposure. What we did in the desert was left there, unlikely to be discovered in the absence of a focused search. And that was the beauty of the wasteland: who would search? Perhaps that is partly why the military was so complacent. The desert can induce an intoxicating liberation upon rational faculties, as if strewing deadly waste among the sagebrush was not much different than tearing off your clothes and running free, exhilarated and ashamed all at once.

Palouse

IN THE SOFT LIGHT OF DUSK, my friend drove me into the empty desert on the outskirts of town. His Volkswagen Beetle hummed along the twists and turns of pavement until he pulled off onto a dirt side road and wound down and around, out of sight. As he turned off the car, my jangly nerves picked up the pace. We walked about fifty feet into a stand of tall grasses, and in the ritual of domesticated dogs, turned a few tight circles to stamp a soft place to sit.

He produced a cellophane bag, tobacco pipe, and lighter, and in a few deft seconds handed me the next decade of my life. Smoke curled from the glowing bowl, and I thought for a moment of the common cup handed to me at communion by the pastor or his assistant so that I could drink the memory of Christ's blood. I wondered if my friend might be the Devil.

After the third lungful of pungent smoke, I exhaled into a world transformed. A small creek of irrigation runoff trickled nearby, and as the drug lifted and opened my mind, the trickle rose into a torrent. I panicked and scrambled away from the threatening water. Then, safely away, each rustle of grass, the fading light of the sky, the dust clinging to my shoes—all of it changed. I changed. A smile formed and from deep within me, from a place I had forgotten or maybe had never known, the purity of joy bubbled over. I giggled. More, I said. Two more deep inhales from the pipe, and I—the protected, anxious, high-school-graduated virgin—knew exhilaration.

I took this turn with no small degree of caution. That spring and summer, most of the friends I hung out with had ventured into this new territory. They grew their own pot on an island in the Yakima River, and the plentiful Tri-Cities sun rewarded them with a prolific crop. At first, blessed with so much bounty, they baked it into brownies. I didn't fully understand what they were doing or how they were affected, as I was yet on the fringes of their budding brotherhood and deep into my own naiveté. They tittered at everything, found the most mundane to be fascinating, but mostly it seemed they were laughing at me. And I could not seem to escape the taunting.

Even a post-graduation family trip to the Midwest pushed the issue in front of me. During a day-visit to old family friends in a Chicago suburb, I found myself in a car with someone I had not seen since childhood. I remembered staying at his house and sleeping with him in his bed the night that my mother and stepdad left on their honeymoon. He had pummeled me while I silently prayed they would return, hope buoyed by each set of headlights that passed by on the road outside. I had forgiven my mother eventually. The friend, I chose to forgive now. He and two friends smoked from a green ceramic elephant bong, inhaling deeply from the end of its trunk. It was the first time I had ever seen marijuana being smoked, and although stung by the exclusion from my friends back home and the isolation of the moment, it was easy to decline participating. Fear held me back. Only days later, in yet another suburb, I was with my cousin and his friends in another car, driving along back roads as they smoked Thai stick from a tiny pipe. Again, I nervously said no as they laughed with red eyes, impressed with the quality of what they had acquired.

Once home from that trip and back among my friends, I gave in because I was invited—into the brotherhood, into a new world. Throughout high school, my timidity crippled any impulses to pursue girls, alcohol, or delinquency. Some saw the fear. Most simply didn't understand me because I wasn't like them. Fear receded in this new world and was immediately replaced by obsession. Nothing in my life leading up to that moment in the tall grass had ever made me feel that humming cocoon of warmth and pleasure. I wanted to feel that way always.

Something else life changing and unexpected happened that night. My senses and awareness, buried under layers of nervous indoctrination, were released. Water, sky, and land were no longer mere wallpaper or mysterious attractions. They became my spiritual partners and places of refuge. This was a new level of experience, a dimension apart from the natural world I observed out of car windows on family trips. Through a magical transformation, I began to see myself in the landscape.

Some of the new connection with nature was a matter of circumstance. I needed to remain hidden to partake in my illegal and morally forbidden pursuit. I had tasted of the fruit of the tree of knowledge, and the landscape that was opened up to me invited me to enter it, away from my parents, my church, my former self. I walked among the sage and Russian olives and along the rocky shores of the Columbia, and I drove on lonely roads far into the undeveloped desert, all to have the separation from civilization that I needed to enter my newly discovered world. The water, rocks, and sage began to speak to me, and I spoke back.

Even away from home, I experienced this altered relationship with nature. During a family trip to Lincoln City, Oregon, with my parents, sisters, and mother's parents, I walked after dinner along the wide, flat beach. On the sand behind a smooth, pale log that had washed ashore, I found shelter from the incessant onshore breeze. Darkness closed around me and steady waves splashed ashore; a full moon ascended from the infinite Pacific and shone down upon me. I implored until I cried, in what amounted to a long, rambling prayer—not to the God I had been trained to worship in church but to the god who drove the waves and lifted the moon, who emanated light in the darkness. "Tell me what I am to do." Whispered, then spoken—shouted in a brave moment—again and again. Those nights I experienced a new side to spirituality, one that cracked open a passage to questions about my purpose. Words from some unnamed source coursed through me, as vital as blood and as unreachable as the stars. And they wanted release.

I had tasted writing now and again in my life but never thought of words as a passage into myself. Instead, they smoothed over my awkwardness with people. When I was sixteen, a junior in high school, the managing editor of our local newspaper turned to my mother one day after church and asked if I would be interested in being a sports stringer. I'd been flipping burgers for a year, so saying yes was easy. I entered a strange world that smelled of newsprint and pulsed to the clatter of teletype machines. My job was to show up at night, when everyone else was gone, to type up bowling scores and answer phone calls—sometimes from coaches, sometimes from people yelling about having missed their paper—and write brief stories. On my first night, a fellow stringer handed me a news release from the publicist of Andre the Giant. The professional wrestler was coming to town for a match. My assignment? Revise the release into a one-paragraph news brief. I labored and agonized for hours. Before long, on twelve-hour Saturdays, I compiled roundups from long, wide ribbons of tele-type paper, using rubber cement and broad grey pencils, marking them up in the language of newspaper editing, then rolling up the finished product and feeding the tube into the pneumatic system. I'd type headlines (1-14-2s: one column, fourteen counts, two lines) on rectangles of pink paper and send them down those same tubes, and sometimes they'd be kicked upstairs by the back shop with a sharp pencil mark indicating that the headline was a count or two long.

Early in that adolescent career, one of the sportswriters who supervised me sent me to cover a basketball game at Burbank High

School, a tiny school in the B classification just outside the Tri-Cities. They were the Coyotes. I walked into a gym shaped like a Quonset hut and sat on bleachers beneath a cobwebbed, stuffed mascot mounted on the wall high above the gym floor. I didn't know what I was doing. So I marked the score sheet I'd been given, drove back to the office after the game, and wrote. The next day, I unfolded the sports section to see my byline and story. Published. I had no idea of the implications.

Nights at the newspaper drew me deeper into a quiet world of green metal desks shoved together in groups—sports over here, news over there, something called the copy desk in the middle. On Friday nights, the stringers were joined by full-time staffers, and on Saturdays the full journalism experience engulfed my senses as the office filled to prepare the Sunday paper. Writers and editors smoked, occasionally showed up drunk, told crude jokes, and spoke loudly about who was sleeping with whom. They yelled, sometimes, once in a while at me. But I returned because somehow I seemed to belong.

Those Friday and Saturday nights allowed me to step away from my high school life. As a writer I could not cheer at the games or show any emotion. They were games that did not involve my own high school's team. While I took notes, my friends cheered somewhere across town. Then they went to dances or parties. My work pushed me into the fringes of their lives. I'd leave the paper at midnight or later, then drive home. Separation grew into isolation. My world became constricted, limited to the newspaper, a few sports writers, and the other stringers with whom I worked.

Still, weeks before graduation, I managed to meet a girl and fall instantly into a gooey pool of infatuation. This was nothing unusual—the falling, that is. I had done it twenty times before with girls I'd never spoken to. But this time, we did speak, and she liked me back.

Pulling into the parking lot of Columbia Basin College, across the river in Pasco, I took the first spot I could find. Orientation started in five minutes. A sign posted at the end of the space declared "Dean." What's a dean? I wondered, then reasoned that school hadn't started yet. Besides, it was a great spot. I guided my recently acquired $600 Chevy Malibu between the lines and went inside feeling pretty good, all things considered. Sure, most of the people I'd known in high school were off to some university somewhere, but a few of my friends stayed behind to attend CBC. An envelope in my pocket contained a check: $1,000 from an office products group. My stepdad's boss brokered my scholarship application and I had been awarded. By my calculations, the money equated to a two-year ride at the community college—tuition, books, and supplies. I was living at home and not asked to pay rent or buy food. That way, I could save for what was next.

I sat through the orientation, certain I was smarter than everyone around me. "Oh, and before I finish," said the presenter, "someone in a white . . . uh, Cougar? Anyway, a white car has parked in the dean's space. You need to move it immediately." Everyone looked around. Red-faced, I arose and walked out, muttering, "Chevy. It's a Chevy."

That is the single clearest memory of the first two-thirds of my freshman year.

I had skipped one class in high school, during the final week of classes, just to see what it felt like. At CBC, I parked in the morning with good intentions, and some days I made my first class. By nine or ten, and occasionally first thing in the morning, I hunched down in a smoke-filled car. It all depended on who had just scored the best weed.

In a magical haze, class schedules faded from relevance. A confluence of forces swept me toward my fate, and I knew it would be a good one. Day after day, I drove along the roads behind the college on the outskirts of the Tri-Cities' small airport or parked by the river, inhaling dreams of my inevitable discovery. Inspired by an English lit class that I rarely attended and didn't completely understand, I began writing poetry glittering with symbolism and clever syntax. As inspiration dawned, I scribbled words down on whatever paper I could find. I'd become teary-eyed at reading them and imagined I was in touch with a deep vein of writerly gold. This, after all, was what great writers did, succumbing to substance abuse and producing brilliant threads of word and thought out of what their minds harvested from the wide sky. I was on the verge of my destiny.

By the end of the quarter, I'd lost track of even what classes were on my schedule. I lived the nightmare of showing up to art history only to realize it was the day of the final, for which I had not prepared. The English lit final left me blank and nonresponsive. For all my burning to write, all I managed to burn was a hole in my Norton anthology with a stray ember from my pipe.

The anonymous generosity of the universe sputtered. After I blew up the engine of my Chevy through abuse and neglect, my father—by himself or with family money—purchased a brand new Ford Pinto as a contribution to my college education. He also called the local police and told them who-knows-what after one of his stepchildren suggested I'd been arrested for smoking pot; the police called my mother and I told her the truth in denial: it was my friend who was busted, not me. And a one-hundred-dollar savings account given to me by my grandmother as an opportunity to demonstrate my fiscal maturity? Whittled to nearly nothing, with no replenishment in sight. I was invited to reapply for a second round of the scholarship; I did so knowing I would be denied.

In history class on the first day of the third quarter, I fumbled with my pen, prepared to take notes. The river called to me with promises of intoxicated inspiration. I watched the professor enter—a small man with an air of intellectual confidence—and sank into my seat. Then he spoke. His words transported me. Oh, he was smart. And he breathed life into the past. I could see the world he described. Feel it. Live in it.

I wanted him to know who I was and that I could appreciate his vision. So I attended, listened, studied. I could not write fast enough during the first blue book exam and filled the pages easily. After a long, desultory departure from being seen as an academic kid, I tasted success once again. Now I could produce a concrete result with words. Not just an A but the highest score in the class. I didn't give up my other obsession. Instead, I managed it, but the balance shifted. Now when I looked out over the landscape, the sky and sage told me there was history to make.

All I knew about the trip to Pullman had been told to me by a muscled college acquaintance with flowing blond locks and a white Corvette. "You can bee-bop up that road," he enthused, adding that a coed prize always awaited him. Other than the knowledge that all two years' worth of my credits would transfer, I didn't have much to go on.

My first trip to Washington State University came the day that my roommate-to-be and I moved there. He drove his mother's Volkswagen van, boxes of secondhand housewares rattling in the back among piles of clothes, towels, and sheets. The narrow two-lane county road escaped the sage-steppe along hills and gullies, winding through the small farm towns of Kahlotus and Washtucna. But nearly two hours into the trip the landscape transformed into a sea of wheat-covered swells. In all directions, all we could see at the top of each rise was the dull gold of wheat or the broken earth of a fallow field.

We were driving on ancient memories of the desert, a rare and prolific example of loess hills, blown there bit by bit over eons. Pullman was merely an island among the windblown detritus of my sandy home—we didn't see it until we crested one final hill.

As we discovered over the next few years, we were never far from the fields, which even a stumbling drunk could find just a few staggering steps from any location on the edge of town, not far beyond campus. I would one day find my blacked-out roommate in one of those fields, locating him by the puffs of breath rising in a column from his mouth as he lay flat on his back in the sub-freezing night.

I arrived at WSU as a communications major but switched to history once I saw the student newspaper. As a veteran of a real newspaper, I believed I had transcended whatever the student version could offer me. Besides, I had become a history junkie, but not as a memorizer of names and dates. The period of the two world wars and the Cold War felt like a time I had already lived through, as if learning more about them amounted to a return to my own past. Studying history expanded my world into a larger context, allowing me to escape the transience of my own short time on this planet. In fact, I believed—reinforced by the half-formed fantasies of my roommate and a few other close friends— that some fate awaited me in history's timeline, and the insularity of Pullman proved an ideal setting for such delusional thoughts to incubate. Moscow, Idaho, lay eight miles away, but it was in the same outer reaches as Pullman. A wide band of oblivion separated their wheat fields and pine covered hills from the rest of the world, and the band grew more immense over time.

Even a crescendo of natural forces conspired to transform Pullman into a surreal experience. In February 1979, a total solar eclipse drew an eerie curtain of shadow and silence over campus. I relished those few moments for the suspension of human activity and the excitement of witnessing a historical event. But I had anticipated the eclipse and planned my participation. I had no idea what would soon be drawn from the drawer of random events.

On May 18, 1980, I sat in my bedroom clacking away at a portable Royal typewriter, desperate to write my final paper for a class in Cuban history. Three roommates and I shared an apartment on a hill on the southeast edge of town. They were outside in the spring weather, having finished, or given up on, their own final projects. When I walked outside to take a break, I saw the leading edge of a dark storm cloud in the wide sky that opened up from the west. Interestingly, though, it seemed to flow from the horizon like a river, a black band meandering through the sky. Not long after I returned to my room to pound the keys for the paper that was going nowhere, one of my roommates burst in. "It's blown!" he said with wide-eyed enthusiasm. "Some chick just ran screaming across the lawn, waving her arms and yelling, 'The volcano has erupted. The volcano has erupted.'"

I went back outside, as if that would tell me something about a mountain exploding on the other side of the state. And it did. The black cloud was no gathering of water vapor. It was a cloud of ash, I realized, moving fast and spreading. A visceral, transcendent tingle froze me in place. By about three that afternoon, the day was as dark as midnight. Large pieces of ash floated to the ground like snowflakes from another planet.

One of my roommates and I huddled under a silvery space blanket and wandered out into a field, shining a flashlight skyward to watch the ash coming down. We returned to our apartment covered in grey powder, and when we tried to rinse the dust out of our hair it nearly turned to concrete. News reports varied wildly—wear a dry scarf over your nose and mouth; no, a damp one; actually, only a surgical mask will work; stay where you are, leave if you can. A knock on our door revealed one of our female neighbors, whom we had never met. She flung her arms around my neck and cried out, "We're having an ash party!" Primal instincts emerged under a volcanic sky.

I peeked through the curtains the next day to see a moonscape: Pullman, covered in grey powder. The next round of unreliable news reports cautioned against driving, but a rumor rendered caution irrelevant. The town was running out of beer. I jumped in my car and made it all of ten feet—the parking lot swirled into a storm of impenetrable dust. I ran the windshield wipers, and the super-fine ash cut a groove into my windshield. Ultimately, my roommate and I donned bandanas around our faces and hiked to the grocery store, returning with cases of beer carried on our shoulders.

I later learned the ash cloud from the cataclysmic explosion traversed most of southern Washington, making deposits at a few high points but merely passing overhead elsewhere—including the Tri-Cities, where a photographer took a picture of the billowing clouds that ended up on the cover of National Geographic. There was no death and destruction in Pullman, only an inconvenient mess. The ash would have to be scooped up and trucked away, much of it used in farmers' fields in the hope of enhancing the soil. After a few days of canceled classes, campus resumed operations, though a few thousand students short. The administration had offered an out to those who felt psychologically threatened or had family in the blast area. They expected a few dozen, not the throngs who lined up for their ticket to escape finals. The rest of us went to class and took our exams, wearing surgical masks while crossing campus. A few weeks later, I graduated with my bachelor's degree in history.

Later that fall, I married that girl who had liked me back—the only serious girlfriend I'd ever had. We moved into a tiny apartment in ramshackle army barracks that had been installed on a golf course in 1945 as temporary housing and had remained ever since. While she pursued a bachelor's degree I attended grad school. More history for me, but without much more direction. A new, talented, and highly demanding faculty member challenged me and I responded, in my way. We drank too much at a conference on diplomatic history and I presented with a hangover, but I presented well. He suggested and supported my application to

Johns Hopkins. I could not imagine I was worthy, nor was I willing to prove it. My life revolved around numbing pain and protecting against emotional loss, at whatever the cost. Unsurprisingly, they turned me down.

I drifted through those years, oblivious of the consequences of inertia, although I suspected then that those major choices of marriage and degree were not really choices at all, but acquiescence to a lack of a better idea. The voice of nature, which had risen into an ethereal chorus my senior year, went silent.

Leaving the Palouse forever meant re-entering the larger world to be husband, worker, full-fledged adult. I had driven those narrow highways dozens of times over the years, but driving them for the final time only to return to the desert felt like surrender. Cowering surrender. The panic attacks had begun during my final semester. The first time, in an economics class delivered in a large lecture hall, I trembled in my seat, convinced I was about to pass out, wet my pants, maybe even lapse into a seizure at the feet of the gathered audience. The waves of throat-constricting terror struck in a grocery store and in the middle of campus.

Back in the Tri-Cities, I awakened from my years-long daydream to find myself sitting in the still familiar newsroom where I had worked before. Same desk, same job. Even the same people, mostly. A full-time sports writing position opened but I failed the screening test miserably, losing out to someone who had just graduated from journalism school. In that room of beat-up desks and hard-won cynicism, I was overeducated and aimless, and I had no idea what to do about it. And back on the wide-open plateau, without the cushion of the Palouse, the landscape whispered in conspiratorial tones. I saw threats in every shadow. Being alone produced the same knee-bending reaction of dizzy breathlessness I was experiencing in public places. The Blue Bridge arced into a desperate fear of falling—from that height, the river wanted only to draw me into its icy heart.

Return also meant a renewed, concerted dedication to avoidance. Five years in Pullman formalized the distancing from my parents—natural enough, even healthy—but to this I added a more forced application of independence. I did not go to the farm or the apartment, and the Cascades stood as a boundary—my side, your side. But that simply reflected the transformation of the world into a stark formula: me, and everyone else. My journey into withdrawal.

ℒ

A few nights before my twenty-fifth birthday, I sat in my dark living room. Normally, I would be surfing the cable listings to see what movie started around 2 a.m. That's how I spent the post-midnight interregnum between work and sleep since accepting a copy editing job. Working 3 p.m. to midnight, with Wednesdays and Thursdays off, shunted me into the deepest isolation I had ever known. I still drove along the river when I could—walked among the rocks, sat along the shore, asked why it wanted to betray me by collapsing a bridge. A vague longing often rose with the wind as I watched the swirling current of the water. But that night at home, with the weight of a quarter-century crushing down on my history-minded conscience, the longing grew into a torrent of tears. I blubbered like a fool as I scrambled for a notebook and pen. The words that emerged have long been lost—too many moves, too many purges—but they seared themselves onto the page: I must write. There is nothing else.

A Gentile in the Wilderness

BEN LOMOND, A SENTRY WITH THE PATIENCE OF STONE, welcomed me as yet another refugee rejected and compelled to find a place to call home. That pyramidal peak atop the Wasatch had caught my eye as I passed it at the north end of Ogden, and I couldn't get it out of my mind.

I couldn't see the peak while sitting next to a ditch of a stream outside a room at the Millstream Motel. But I imagined it as I looked up at the benches of the mountain range and silently asked them to reveal my fate. I searched for a response among steep, crumbling slopes that sported a five o'clock shadow of scrub oak and a thin memory of geological shoreline from a near-dead lake. In the harsh evening light of my first night in Utah, with the sun glowering over the west desert, the mountains accepted the aspirations of a wannabe writer, husband, man. I listened carefully to my heart. My head, as usual, abstained.

The trip itself hadn't been necessary because I'd already been offered a job over the phone: copy editor for the local newspaper. But I couldn't bring myself to accept it without having seen the place. Those sorts of details were far from my mind when I placed a classified ad in *Editor & Publisher*, "copy editor for hire." Two newspapers replied, and this one, in Ogden, promised a day shift. That's all I sought. More than four years of swing shift had left my marriage in tatters. At least, the work schedule was something external to blame. Far too easily in my wired post-shift hours, the newspaper put to bed, I rediscovered the predawn landscape of the

Tri-Cities, which had not so many years before been my personal cloaking device, concealing me and the life I was living.

So I drove down with my wife. I toured the paper and lunched with the staff. Then, after investigating a few neighborhoods, I sat outside the hotel room. Except for the place of my birth, which I left pre-memory, I had not lived in another state and certainly never considered living in Utah. I called the paper back and said yes.

Within a year, I was divorced, broke, and alone. In Utah.

Strains of Patsy Cline wailing through the duplex walls meant that my German neighbor's Mexican boyfriend had punched her again. Or cheated on her. Or (briefly) left her. In the aftermath, she always turned to Patsy.

I stepped outside to do what I always did just beyond the door: gaze at the mountains. I didn't hold anything against them. They hadn't lied. I simply hadn't received the message correctly, and from my now-bachelor half of the duplex in the southeast part of town I still enjoyed looking due west at the rising slopes and north at Ben Lomond Mountain. Still with appreciation for the beauty, in awe of their presence, and with supplication in my soul. I could count on the mountains being there, in the same way that I once counted on the Columbia.

One house over, two daughters of Italian descent, and the boyfriend of one of them, lived together. From their wide back deck, the crinkling of an empty beer can or the tinkle of ice in a bourbon-and-water was as common as a call from a suburban sparrow. Beyond this multicultural microcosm, I had not developed much of an idea about where I lived. As the wire editor at the newspaper, I read plenty of local stories, but the green text on the word processing screen was abstract. I needed to get out more.

After a year, I still didn't know much about Mormons. They were, I recalled, responsible for the two young men in white shirts who visited my stepfather once a month or so in our Kennewick home when I was a child. I didn't listen to what they talked about, although my conservative Christian mother did and argued with them often. They showed up with an envelope in hand, the type fastened with a string, and they expected it to contain money when they left. This I resented because we had no money, and any that went to the church was supposed to go to our church, the Lutheran one.

Even as I emerged from my post-divorce emotional exile, most of my daily exposure to Mormonism came in the form of anti or ex. There were no-longer-practicing Mormons or go-to-church-for-a-christening Mormons. At the newspaper, I met a few outright dissidents. They were my kind of people, and I became increasingly proud of my affiliation with them. We were misfits, drinking, smoking, cohabitating, and generally not conforming to local culture. One couple, a photographer and a reporter, lived together in an apartment that featured, on the outside of the front door, a portrait of the prophet (a.k.a. church leader) with a piece of gray duct tape placed over his mouth. This symbol marked a place of sanctuary.

In public, I traversed a world that seemed to be on drugs, although I could never find any myself. It was a world crowded with ironic juxtapositions. The pressure to marry young and the prevalence of divorce. Clean-cut suburbanites and rough-cut rednecks, their golf-course lawns and broken-down mobile homes invisible to one another but only a neighborhood away. A church building across from every public school and some of the lowest spending per pupil in the nation. Everywhere smiles and happy faces, and inordinately high rates of suicide and drug abuse. And as I began to raise these points to people I met, I heard more than once these precise words: "If you don't like it here, then get out. This is our state."

Just because advice is issued with malice, that doesn't make it bad. But I didn't listen.

We met at a party, I went home with her, and so began a tumultuous, eventful, brief relationship and marriage. The next morning, she drove me from her Sugar House neighborhood in Salt Lake City along Highway 89, which traversed the benches of the Wasatch at about the level of the ancient shores of Lake Bonneville. It was known as the mountain road. Over the next few months, the mountains and I conversed while I looked out over the Great Salt Lake to the west. I spent so much time with my eyes on the mountains and the lake that I'm surprised I never left the road, and I am probably lucky to have never hit one of the deer that, hit by others, littered the highway's shoulders. That drive, south in the afternoons and early evenings, then north usually before dawn, was more of a communal experience than it was a commute, and if I had understood that better, or understood myself at all, I would simply have made the drive and forgotten about the rest. I loved to be alone in my car but didn't know how to be alone in life. There wasn't enough of a well-formed me to stand apart from another.

Riding in a converted school bus full of hikers and camping equipment, I wondered if I had finally found a pathway to accepting where I lived. The landscape had remained out there somewhere, and now I finally took the opportunity to move from child-like appreciation to getting out into the land. We were headed to a spot on the Green River, from which we'd take a gentle ride on bulging rubber rafts. I squirmed in my seat, even though my wife sat next to me—the best attitude I could work up around a bunch of strangers was a half-step just this side of disdain. A few miles into the trip, a thirty-something man with long, straight hair took a guitar out of its case. I winced, expecting bad playing, or worse, bad playing and bad singing. Or the apocalypse: a sing-along. But he played well enough and sang in a gentle drawl that approached being pleasant. The tune put me at ease.

Three hours later, I had fantasized all the ways I could smash the guitar over his head. He had not stopped playing and singing—not all that well, it turned out—and the interior of the bus became so pressurized with exasperation that we spilled out upon arrival, gasping for a quiet moment. Within the hour, we had pitched our tents, and from within one of them I heard the click of a guitar case opening, followed by an introductory strum. The dirge began anew. Only during the tent pitching did we realize he was on the trip with a woman, who solemnly assisted with setting their camp. By morning, she was gone. No one was sure by what means she had escaped. We did not hear another song the rest of the weekend.

Without the pervasive soundtrack, it was possible, even with so many people, to find moments in which the gentle lapping of the river against the shore, or a fleeting breeze through the pines, or the chirping of a territorial chipmunk could prevail. I welcomed the comfort afforded by the presence of others but wished for their silence around the campfire that night, so that I could listen to the crackle of burning wood, and on the rafts the next day, so that the river could speak uninterrupted.

I did not find peace on that trip or hear a reassuring message about being home. What I felt was between—on my way from something, on my way to something. Open to change. I was married to someone ten years older with two children who invited me into their home, but I was a traveler and I knew it, and I believe they knew it. She embraced a message of awakening, yet her stern "that stops now" ended, without ceremony, my long, smoky journey through self-medication.

A petty dispute set in motion the final break with my father. I offended him with a snub—refusing to show up at his house when he expected me to be there. Instead, a week later I wrote him a letter. It may have been the only time I ever wrote him. I tried to be wise and compassionate while not flinching. In response, I heard his voice for the final time when I played a message on an answering machine. Orders. Commands. Deadlines.

I listened to it all and I had heard enough. For that time. For a lifetime. I left him in silence, permanent and complete, the coldest revenge I could contrive. His world and mine would never intersect again.

Looking up at the benches, across the mountain highway, I considered the questions I had asked them five years earlier. I still believed the mountains meant to tell me something. One of my brothers-in-law strolled past on his way to the pool. A sculpted yard lay between the water and a privacy-ensuring stand of scrub oak. Behind me, in the suburban mansion, was my wife. I was surprised that her family had been willing to accept me, that anyone would take me in so easily in such circumstances: after a second divorce, sleeping on the floor of a friend's apartment, pulling my clothes out of plastic garbage bags because I had no place else to put them. I wondered if the mountains were laughing at me, just a little.

After the expensive wedding, the Hawaiian honeymoon, the family trips to conventions and big-city long weekends, I looked up at the Wasatch mostly with the concern that I did not belong. Visiting the home of my in-laws exhumed the humiliation of discovering that one of the boys I knew in middle school—the son of a Hanford engineer—had frequently invited me to his house-with-a-pool and took me on water ski trips only because his mother, in some Christian exercise of service to the less fortunate, had ordered him to. That lesson in unworthiness had stuck.

My wife was the smartest person I'd ever met, an ex-pat from her own religion, and I was under the impression she was nearly as hopeless at relationships as I was. The ways of the universe being a mystery, I decided to leave a little less to fate and conform myself to the mold of a professional, proper, well-behaved adult. That would be something new.

We bought the final treeless half-acre lot available in an established neighborhood a block away from Gentile Street, placing us and her three siblings and her parents within a circle of just a few miles. Thus ensued a battle with landscape that would begin shaping my views on the matter of development. To that point in my life, watching heavy equipment shape an unruly parcel into a smooth patch of dirt aroused no sense of violation. A foundation is poured, boards begin to rise from the concrete, and a building replaces an empty lot. Natural enough.

My long lesson began in earnest when two semitrucks with flat-bed trailers groaning under the weight of sod-laden pallets pulled up in front of the newly built home. They held enough sod to cover nineteen thousand square feet, most of which was in the backyard. That configuration—even the choice of that lot—had been a concession to my desire for space. Literal distance between me and any neighbors. I joked about someday owning a "naked coffee" home, in which I could have a cup on my back deck in my natural state and not be seen. This was not such a house, but at least the neighbors in back were across the way, not just over the fence. Taming all that spaciousness with a golf-course lawn was the only option I understood. The neighborhood featured virtual fairways between the houses, all meticulously groomed, watered, and fertilized. It did not cross my mind that this was a high desert. That the home had been built on an ancient lakebed, which was merely a thin layer of poor topsoil splotched like pancake makeup over a deep bed of hard clay. Somehow I naively imagined that carving trenches for an underground sprinkler system and awkwardly plopping rectangular cuts of sod onto the dusty soil would manifest the seamless greenery I saw all around the rest of the neighborhood.

Conformity exacted a high price. The landscaping project became an epic struggle. A line of lilacs across the back of the property wilted from over watering. Large patches of grass withered from under watering. Sprinkler pipes leaked. The merciless and unbroken west-setting sun fried a manufactured hillside planted with juniper shrubs and phlox. A river birch slowly died for reasons that were not apparent until, one day, a mysterious dampness spread across the concrete floor of a lower-level room. We called the contractor, who showed up quickly and drilled a hole in the side of the floor drain. A stream of water shot out from the hole. "Uh oh," was all he said. Hours later, as a backhoe scooped away dirt from the southwest corner of the foundation, a geyser erupted. Underground springs snaked their way from the benches to the lake, drawing water from above in dry times, transporting water down from the mountains in wet ones. We had built over the top of one, and when I dug up the dead birch, its roots were at once rotted by the excess water and choked from being unable to navigate the surrounding hard clay.

In response, I hurled myself at the yard. I lashed at it. I seethed. But the yard refused to submit. Futility is the patient work of fate.

When we first moved in, none of this conflict seemed inevitable. Pies and plates of cookies were left on our front doorstep as anonymous gifts. People would stop by just to introduce themselves and say hello. That our street address was a compass point coordinate seemed quirky but not imbued with deeper significance. But this was how the Mormon settlers had laid out their plats. Before long, the gifts and visits stopped. Admittedly, such would be the case in just about anyplace where these sorts of greetings are a part of the culture. At that point, the newcomer either joins the community or chooses instead to live in isolation. But there is nothing quite like the isolation that comes with being a Gentile in Utah.

The pervasiveness of churches; the restriction to 3.2 beer in grocery stores; the complicated and ritualistic procedures for purchasing hard liquor at a restaurant; the infusion of the church's opinion into public and political matters, and thus into the media;

the ubiquitous image of young, pregnant mothers with a baby in arms and two or more children in tow, pushing a shopping cart or piling into a hulking SUV (or MAV: Mormon Assault Vehicle). I could see that Utah itself was in isolation, despite the world-domination outlook of its most ardent adherents. In the Salt Lake City International Airport, where welcoming celebrations for returning missionaries are common occurrences, I overheard a young woman telling her friend as she pointed to a world map of Mormon missionary enclaves unfolded on their laps, "First we'll take Russia, and then England, and then the rest of Europe, and South America . . ."

I grimaced. Helplessness crawled around in my gut. I was a stranger in a strange land. The son-in-law hanger-on of a well-to-do family.

୬

When my former college roommate called—my long-lost friend, the boy whose birthday was a day after mine, who dreamed the biggest of our shared dreams and painted the most spectacular of our delusions—I awkwardly played my phone conversation role. Awkward mostly because I could not stay in touch, could not make one damned effort to maintain ties to him or anyone. But I missed him and told him so.

We talked about his life. He'd become a runner. Lost all that weight from college, recovered from an addiction to alcohol. He was running, and he was on his way. And me? Oh, just working at a newspaper. Hapless but hopeful in the realm of relationships. And sure. Absolutely. I would stay in touch.

His call was still fresh in my mind, as were my intentions to renew our friendship, the day not so much later that another old friend called.

"Did you have a good talk?" he asked.

"Yeah," I said. "We did."

"Good. Because he's gone."

Hit by a car while out running. Died instantly.

A few days later, I was told there would be a wake. All the old gang would be there. I hesitated. I'd just accepted a job as sports editor. I'd manage people, write a column, cover NBA games. I had responsibilities. I couldn't simply leave.

So I didn't go, and instantly hated not going. (About twenty years later, I would go—to the memorial and wake for the friend who'd called with the news, and who also died suddenly and unexpectedly.) Instead, I remained, convinced that I needed to learn how. Utah became my court-ordered ankle bracelet. I could travel to Hawaii or Chicago or San Francisco, could visit, as a popular T-shirt noted, the fun places in Utah: Evanston, Wyoming, for horse racing; Burley, Idaho, to buy a lotto ticket; and Wendover, bifurcated by the Nevada-Utah border, with gambling on one side of town but not the other. But always, ineluctably, I returned.

The Pit from Thirty Thousand Feet

MY NEW LIFE DAWNED ON THE ROAD. The ten-hour drive connecting the Tri-Cites to northern Utah always provided plenty of time for thought and reflection about who and where I was. No firm answer ever appeared but being able to drive to Washington in a day reinforced the idea that home was still a reachable place.

The desert could still draw me away from Utah, pulling me onto I-15 north out of Ogden. As the top end of the Wasatch Range rose within reach I could sense the Idaho border—a deceptive but immediate gratification. Distance. Once pointed due northwest on Highway 84, with the mountains full in my rearview mirror and the Great Basin opening up before me, I focused on home, anticipating the markers of the trip that would come. The unpopulated sage-pocked corridor between Black Pine Peak and the Sublett Range. The long city-skirting stretch of 84 from Twin Falls to Boise, tantalizingly close to the Snake River, which except for two quick crossings near Mountain Home existed only as an idea somewhere deep within a channel whose ancient banks traced ironically across parched, brown earth.

Then the anticipation of another crossing, now into Oregon, again back on a northwesterly tack, a course set for the Blue Mountains. Their ethereal appearance on the Tri-Cities horizon had always symbolized for me the uncertain allure of a world beyond, so to approach them from the other side aroused a sense of entering the mist so that I could emerge into a landscape of familiarity. This is the most beautiful part of the drive, the twenty-five miles from Baker to La Grande, where tall pines and surrounding mountains evoked powerful childhood memories of the Cascades. (And where once a near collision with a huge elk crossing the freeway reminded me of my transience in the continuum of nature.) But the joy is ephemeral, as it was in my youth. Already by Pendleton, another twenty-five miles beyond La Grande, change fills the air, and just beyond town stands a demarcation as dramatic as the bisection that marked east from west in Washington. The precipitous, twisting descent, marked by dozens of warning signs to truckers and escape ramps when the signs become irrelevant, is dramatic enough, but inescapable is the understanding that here lies a separate place—a place in which the majority of my life had unfolded. At one sweeping turn at the top of the grade, the expansive, dry, flat basin of southeastern Washington simply emerges as an anti-mirage, with a horizon that defies definition—a place in which a traveler could disappear forever.

At the bottom, nostrils fill with the metallic pungency of smoking brakes, and the temperature is higher, the air drier and hazier. Dust pervades the atmosphere. A patchwork of irrigated farmland breaks the landscape into pockets of shrub-steppe. The tops of two bridges hint of the wide Columbia, which wears the Tri-Cities like a set of light summer clothes. The return trip south passes in a blur with little to anticipate except the end of the drive—by then, my love for being behind the wheel would finally have dissipated into weariness.

But on this trip, I was looking forward into the unknown. A few weeks before, an acquaintance of mine from work had suggested that I needed help. That I was not just down but clinically depressed, and only serious, professional intervention could make a difference. I didn't argue. The inciting incident was an office Halloween party. I'd worn a rubber mask pulled completely over my head and haunted the party as a mute monster. But when the party was over, I left the mask on and still refused to speak. I couldn't come out.

So I took the advice, visited my doctor, filled out a bubble-sheet questionnaire, and emerged with a trial prescription of Prozac. The drug would take two weeks or more to take effect, which I found unsatisfying because in the past my drugs of choice took effect immediately. I brought the box of pills with me on a visit home for Thanksgiving and secretly began taking them there, reminded of when I was younger—grade school, perhaps—and the doctor sent me and my mother home with a sample bottle of tiny white phenobarbital pills for those mysterious pains that slashed through my sides when worries about my world grew too intense.

Those pills from childhood never made any difference that I could tell. And as I drove back to Utah, I wondered if the same would be true again. One mile emptily linked to another mile, one hour passed like any other hour. Then everything changed.

Everything. All of it. A tingling sensation swept over me as if a sticky film had just been peeled off my brain and the light came streaming in.

Time, place, perception, mood—I simply stopped being who I had been all my life and became someone I did not know. Oh, the joy! I nearly ascended from my seat behind the wheel. In that first instant, I saw the clouds. Not the gray, flat blotches that had been passing along overhead. No, they now had intricate form and dimension and detail, and they soared, and I soared with them. My heart raced. Gray tattooed my soul and white exploded with the power of religion. The sky opened up into a transit between galaxies. Over the next few hours, intense sensations swept over me like waves crashing onto a beach.

That night, as I failed to sleep, I realized that the ache in my head was from the frozen spasm of a smile that had, from that moment on the road, been splashed across my face.

It was the beginning of the beginning, and if only it could have remained so.

Two more meds soon supplemented my Prozac high. Now certain of my imperviousness to the forces of depression and anxiety, I felt the invincibility that might have filled me when I was a teenager, had I not been so timid. The timing was at once thrilling and ominous. For that fateful office party had not been at the newspaper. I had left that place, and the entire failing industry, behind with a gut full of bitterness over furloughs and internal politics. The gig had rekindled the dormant writer within as I produced a weekly column and covered NBA games. But inadequacy still gnawed at me. I was still just a sportswriter. In my new job, I worked as a writer and editor in the corporate office of a government contractor. The business operated Job Corps centers—a federal program of education and job training for disadvantaged youth. The centers were scattered across the country, which meant I would travel.

My primary call to action was to serve as the in-house editor and write magazine articles while raising the writing skills of corporate staff. After many months of this—and after the mental health intervention—they asked if I could teach business writing to line staff. I said I could do it, although I had never done such a thing. But under the influence of my meds, I was brimming. An ego on steroids. Flying across the country to Brunswick, Georgia; or Philadelphia; or Denison, Iowa, as the guy from corporate drew an intoxicating level of attention. People were nice to me, even deferential. On the road, I could be the kind of person I'd always envied. This new person could try on new places, and finding the next place—beyond Utah—became an obsession. Yet anticipation collapsed into disappointment as I discovered the fatal flaw that would not allow me to live in each new place. Time after time, my exhilaration inevitably settled into despair and deepened the emptiness I brought with me.

My newfound confidence drew me out of hotel rooms to explore the surrounding area, but it didn't drive me into anything. The farther afield I wandered, the more I walked the streets, the more I understood I was alone.

While riding a tour tram in Washington, DC, I regarded the passing landscape as if it were a movie screen. Rolling past the National Cathedral or Ford's Theatre, stepping off to walk up to the Lincoln Memorial or through Arlington Cemetery, watching the flame flicker over the Kennedy graves, I opened myself to the confluence of past and present, hoping for resonance. Nothing. The vibration of their significance passed by me, not through me.

The highs grew sharper, the lows deeper. The cycling swirled into a storm of behavior with its own momentum. I made poor decisions or none at all. My sins were legion. (I? My? Some person I'd kept locked and hidden busted out and swept away the scaffolding of guilt and conscience. No thought, only action.)

In such a state, only the absurd could slow me down long enough to capture my attention.

❧

I'd been to Brunswick before, so when a coworker asked about a day trip, I welcomed a break from town. When she suggested Okefenokee swamp, I responded with skepticism.

"Isn't that in a cartoon?"

"A comic strip," she replied. "But it's a real place."

"You know this for sure?"

"No. Well, I saw a brochure, I think. Let's go. I'll drive."

That was enough for me. I watched as the highway cut through pervasive greenery that washed over the landscape. Road signs indicated that this was a hurricane evacuation route. Something about a surge. It surprised me to see such signs so far inland on the road to Waycross.

We arrived at Okefenokee to copious signage of a different sort. These were warnings, making clear that the immediate surroundings were not a national forest or park. They explained that alligators wandered the grounds freely, and that alligators are dangerous. Trying to imagine who would need to be told that, I carefully considered the "freely" part. Another sign: if an alligator is blocking the path you are on, then choose another path. Yes, of course. If only our obstacles in life were so obvious, and our choices so clear.

My coworker went her way and I went mine. Not yet twenty cautious steps from the parking lot, I encountered an eight-foot gator on a footpath. It was being fed a cheeseburger by a leering tourist—sixtyish and mostly bald, spindly white legs poked into black leather loafers, his yellow cotton polo stretched like a balloon over a protruding belly. As a few visitors, myself included, watched from a safe but curious distance, he tore off another chunk from within the crinkled wrapper and tossed it to the gulping gator, standing close enough to display his sheer obliviousness to the concept of proximity and the impending moment when the cheeseburger wrapper was empty. I did not stay to see it, disgusted by the human capacity for ignoring reasonable rules and corrupting the innocent.

After a few more random encounters, I purchased a ticket for a raft ride. The inflatable promised to take a small group of us into the very swamp itself, moving slowly through channels of still water with banks on each side close enough to be touched by an oar. The ride began comfortably uneventful, as our guide drawled his scripted comments about the flora and fauna and recounted a brief history of the swamp over the muted hum of a small electric-powered propeller. Rounding one lazy bend, however, we could see a very large—certainly more than eight-foot-long—gator, and as the guide droned, our little boat approached it. As if we were in Disneyland, the guide seamlessly wove the beast into his dialogue, explaining that she was a momma and that this was a time of year not to gratuitously test her patience. She stood on the bank, parallel to the channel, a rugged, deep green, maternal sentry. I studied her respectfully. Just as we pulled alongside, her jaws flung open to a collective gasp, and she hissed with primordial sincerity, invoking in me a fleeting understanding of death by large amphibian.

The place had my attention. I continued to look and listen, learning a little more about the thick tendrils of cypress roots reaching from the brackish water and the Spanish moss draped on twisted branches overhead. In the end, I consummated the visit in my own tourist's fashion, purchasing a T-shirt with an alligator emblazoned on the front, with the intention to wear it and remind myself that indeed, I had been to Okefenokee, and it was real.

My day began in a cubicle, ground zero for the routine of a corporate drone. I'd moved downstairs at headquarters to move up in the world, now as a writer and editor in the realm of private corrections. I had no idea exactly how that would work. The future of this business line seemed a bright one, although I had much work to become acclimated to ex-cops and ex-wardens, all of them ex-military, and none of them acutely aware of the meaning of *ex*.

A phone rang. The manager who answered it went a little pale, then said with energy, "There's been an incident."

I listened from a few desks away. A correctional facility in California. Rocks were thrown. A lockdown. Media would be on their way. Then the attention turned to me: "Get on the first available flight," a director told me.

I rushed home and feverishly packed, remembering to put the folder that contained what I would need to know about Eagle Mountain in my carry-on bag. Once on the plane, I studied the map I'd been given. Eagle Mountain lay ten miles north of Interstate 10, which runs from LA to Phoenix, on the edge of Joshua Tree National Park and in the midst of isolated mountain ranges—Eagle, Coxcomb, Pinto, and a dozen others—on a high desert plateau.

I would not be alone on this trip. One of my new coworkers would also go, an ex-Marine and former employee of the Texas Department of Criminal Justice.

"Lemme tell you how they do it at the TDCJ," he would say with a subtle Texas twang, to emphasize how things are done when they are done properly.

He would form the operational wing of our two-man corporate team, overseeing the transition to stand-down while I deflected the inevitable media curiosity. With expedience being paramount, we traveled separately, each catching whatever flight we could, renting our own cars, and driving our own routes.

After arriving in California, I obsessed with the map. But as the landscape opened up, I realized I would hardly need it. Few roads left even fewer options. There was only one turn after getting on the freeway: left at Desert Center. Before I reached that point, the starkness of the place took me aback, despite my desert roots. In the distance, a sharp line of dark rock arched, ancient and menacing, from the desert floor like the dorsal ridge of a dinosaur. Who could look at that stark, rugged thrust of geological forces and not feel the primitive sense of that place? Just a mile off the highway, life could be measured by a canteen of water.

I witnessed a paucity of civilization and a surfeit of earth desperate for water and hardened by the lack of it. They were strangely attractive ideas. I mused that most of the people who lived there must do so willingly because it was no place for a commoner or a common life. Or perhaps common life had no use for them. This was no one's backyard.

But as my corporate partner and I converged, I understood that this trip would be profoundly different from anything I had experienced before. When I arrived at Eagle Mountain, the force of bewilderment raised my foot from the gas pedal. I would be staying in a ghost town. Not piles of rocks that required a brochure to explain, or an Old West tourist trap. Instead, neighborhoods of modest 1960s-style ranch homes neatly arranged within a gently flowing network of residential streets. The faded pastels of their exteriors showed little other wear. But boards of plywood covered every window and door of every house. The movie theater, the grocery store. Everything was there but not there. And now, dutifully following the street-level directions I had been given, I navigated my way to a house that was not boarded, where I would be staying for the next few days with Mr. TDCJ.

I unpacked, slowly unfolding into the strangeness of my sentience amidst the ethereal residents, whom I could sense all around. When he arrived, he sat his ridiculously small bag, hardly more than a satchel, on a bed and proceeded to produce a week's worth of perfectly folded, unwrinkled dress shirts and pants, which from their hangers mocked my meager, motley assortment of barely business-casual clothes.

"How the heck did you do that?" I asked, motioning to his closet.

"A Marine is always ready," he said, beaming with the anticipation of work to be done.

Within an hour, we drove past more abandoned homes, one final bend in the street, and then saw the facility: white, squarish buildings, sequestered within an enclave of undeveloped land pocked with clumps of desert grasses. A tall fence topped with razor wire, sentries in a tower; otherwise, no evidence of people. Lockdown. Even from the public parking lot I sensed the transition from outside to inside. A guard greeted us, mentioning a sniper perimeter.

"Oh, where is it?" I asked.

He grinned. "You're in it," he said, motioning to a ridge of rocks a hundred yards in the distance.

Already unsettled, I was escorted past a tall fence to an open area, where guards held shotguns in their folded arms or paced with German shepherds on taut leashes. I had entered yet another strange land. Although the inmates were confined to quarters, this was my first true experience with the landscape of incarceration.

(Notwithstanding our eighth-grade trip to the maximum security state prison in Walla Walla, Washington, from which I remember a leering guard answering a question about gas chambers by saying, "Nope, we hang 'em here.") This world-within-a-world felt nothing like an island, imbued with the exotic sense of sublime separation—almost a lifting up, not just away, from the weight of life on the continent. Instead, this place felt contained. A world unto itself. Even the sniper monitored us from another dimension. His bullet would be as unexpected and impersonal, if not as random, as a meteorite plunging from the depths of space.

The body of my work consisted of writing a press release, as much to comfort the warden as to offer any substantive fodder for the media, and to intercept a reporter and camera man from Palm Springs in the parking lot, where I answered in a calm and informative way questions about violence, racism, and the general safety of the public. As if there were enough of the public close enough to care about what happened.

This left me with plenty of time to discover more about the place outside the fence. I walked alone among the houses, my mind filling with images of the people who had lived there. How they lived, and what it would be like to live in a place like this. One theater, one store, one extended neighborhood, really, with no visible sense of economic disparity. Community. I wondered if the scene was so idyllic because of the lack of people. The ones in my imagination may have been nothing like the ones who actually lived there; perhaps I imagined a community that could never exist, that had never existed. But I was the only one on those streets. Being a student of history, I projected that perspective into entropy. How long until all that remains is incomplete foundations and crumbled asphalt bordered by disintegrating concrete curbs? I had for my reference point only the scantest of evidence: a partial foundation or the last remnants of a rock fireplace at scattered sites around the Tri-Cities. Like a single bone of a giant dinosaur, they told one small piece of a rich story, and as a young boy I eagerly filled in the details. I learned later that the ghost town of Patterson did indeed exist near the Snake River close to Burbank, and as for the rest of the detritus of human settlement that I saw, I never sought nor did I hear of any explanation of origins or demise. What I could imagine was history enough for me.

At Eagle Mountain, though, a full history lesson was in the offing. Near the end of my visit, I was given an official tour of the place—a former Kaiser copper mine that now sat as empty as the town, only on a scale of emptiness that evoked awe for the works that humans will endeavor to undertake. The guide, a middle-aged woman, might well have been the corporeal embodiment of the collective souls of Eagle Mountain. Our tour did not take us to the pit itself but drove along gravel roads among massive piles of rocks and machinery so large that it could clearly serve no other purpose than to stand and rust where it stopped, with no more earth to dig and no more slag to scoop and drop. The guide spoke with as much hope as reminiscence, weaving into explanations of the operation her sincere vision of how the place could soon become the largest garbage heap on the planet, with the stuff rolling in on trains and going into a hole that would take a century to fill. Her gray eyes glinted with the anticipation of life returning to Eagle Mountain, the boards coming down and the houses being occupied again. What I saw as only the past inevitably becoming the deeper past, she saw as the future.

When finally I left Eagle Mountain, I did not want to go. Yet I also knew that I would never fully leave the place. Or that it would not leave me. In those vacant streets, I felt eerily welcome, convinced that someday I would return—that I would be compelled to, in this life or in another.

Virgin Territory

I BEGAN PSYCHOTHERAPY with a simple proposition.

"My life is completely out of control," I said from the comfort of a leather couch in an office in Salt Lake City, and catalogued the evidence as the doctor listened. I thought it was a rather impressive list. She didn't flinch.

"I think I've been at this place before. Last time, I crashed and burned. I don't want to do that again."

Partially true. The med-induced swings of emotion and behavior were not anything I'd previously experienced. My well-intentioned and likeable family doc had given me a gallon of gasoline to go with a box of matches, and my self-directed attempt to clear out the brush was burning down the neighborhood. So the feeling that I'd gotten myself into an untenable situation—a mess of circumstance, consequence, and confusion—yes, that seemed entirely familiar.

She carefully explained that we would begin at the beginning, and it would take time, and I could say anything. Anything. So I did. I yelled back at my father, freed my conscience from my mother's, separated choice and free will from sin, and took responsibility in place of blame. Of all the confessions and discoveries from as far back as I could remember, one event shone as the moment the universe paused just long enough for me to catch a glimpse of my proper place in it.

∂

My mother's father had retired early after being injured as a firefighter, so he and my grandma traveled the country, camping in parks, fishing in lakes and rivers, living the landscape. Grandma recorded a few details about the weather in a journal every day for decades. They learned all they could about the places they visited. Grandpa was obsessive about knowledge, so every rock, tree, and creature he came across became a subject for intense study, in person and out of books. He had trapped snapping turtles in Minnesota and fished for grouper in Lake Okeechobee. He had been stung by a Portuguese man-of-war in the surf in Florida and walked within yards of a coiled rattlesnake in Arizona. When they lived for a time in a small trailer outside of Tucson, he and my grandmother used broomsticks to poke tarantulas out of a cinder block wall next to their driveway. They shook out their shoes in the morning to check for scorpions.

I know I'd invoked that lifestyle at some point after beginning my corporate travel because my wife told me, "You can't live like that." Modestly, with a guaranteed income, free to travel, read, write, and play. I had to accept her premise—that with no pension or disability payment, I was not in my grandfather's financial situation. But the rest haunted me.

When Grandpa dropped to the floor in the midst of a heart attack, Grandma—who hadn't driven in years—got him to the hospital. We marveled at her determination, then at his as he recovered from a quadruple bypass. Afterward, I visited them at their trailer park in Las Vegas, where they had settled down to stay after all that wandering. He lamented over a plate of scrambled egg whites and low-cholesterol turkey bacon that his chess game, and his memory in general, would never be the same after the surgery. I assured him, and myself, that he'd be fine.

When my mother called to say he was back in the hospital, this time with pneumonia, I assured her, and myself, that he'd get through it. But the phone calls kept coming. She described how ill he had become and how much weight he had lost. She was getting tired. I volunteered to make the drive south so she could have a break.

Even with all the landscape for my mind to wander over during seven hours of driving, I wasn't ready. I had imagined a pale grandpa or a sorrowful one. I pictured pallor and wrinkles and suffering eyes. As soon as I walked into the room, cautiously breathing vapid hospital air, my lungs struggled with the emptiness of despair. There in the hospital bed I saw death layered over him like a blanket of decay—sunken cheeks, bulging eyes, protruding nose, mouth agape.

I failed to hide my shock. I'll never know if he noticed. When I walked out of that room, I did so with relief. I would need time to comprehend what was happening. A white plastic bulletin board hung on the wall next to Grandpa's room. Written on it in blue ink were the words, "Today is April 1, Good Friday." I stared at the message, remembering all the Good Fridays of my church-going past, when we pulled black shrouds over the stained glass windows and left at the end of the service in silence. And so I walked out of his room in silence, and for his sake I wanted to shroud the window and hide in the darkness what my eyes could hardly bear to see. To hide the truth I knew in my heart.

In the desert, the sun swaggers like a bully. Even in April the southern Nevada sky is barely big enough to hold all the light. I could block out the sun itself with my hand but that didn't stop it from beating down on me. So I felt small, driving to calm myself on the next afternoon. Yet that's how it is in the West. Driving seven or ten or twelve hours is nothing unusual. The expanse demands patience as a price to cross it and I gladly paid because the territory gave me wide, empty space for my pent-up soul to unfold. I cruised north along the Boulder Highway back toward Las Vegas, trying to open the box I'd been stuffed in and to get that sickening, sterile hospital smell out of my mind.

A semitruck whooshed past heading south. It reminded me to pay at least a little attention to the road, though my mind was out there, soaring over the land like a hawk looking for a meal—but with all that damn sun I couldn't see a thing. I rubbed my forehead and blinked away tears. Conscious once again of the road, I wondered how much time had just passed. Nothing much had changed on either side of the road, and the way ahead remained a gray line extending into the limbo of wasteland, promising a destination beyond the horizon of my vision.

Snapped out of distraction by a peripheral change in the horizon, I noticed a casino hulking above the sagebrush ahead. The architectural nightmare rose out of the desert floor as I approached, its huge flashing sign proclaiming loose slots and $4.99 prime rib dinners. Sunlight glinted off car windows in the five-acre parking lot. Another casino appeared on the horizon, on the other side of the highway. The word "KENO" in ten-foot-high black letters beckoned travelers before they could even make out much of the building itself. I wondered why anyone would stop at such cheap imitations before they arrived at the real thing. Then again, the word "real" doesn't have much value when applied to Las Vegas.

Soon I saw the uneven Vegas skyline cutting across a tangerine dusk. Within a mile or two concrete and glass consumed sagebrush and Joshua trees. A gaudy architectural buffet, the urban skyline contrasted remarkably with its ascetic, arid backdrop. Which was to the city's advantage; temptation blossomed from the desert's stark pallet. Even if you're prepared, the leap is a little much. Just how many lights and sounds and varieties of stimulation can be processed all at once? Vegas swallows even the hard-bitten hedonist. A prophet emerging from the desert after two decades of fasting and prayer would turn back, knowing all the signs of a lost cause. Even the open sky was not immune to architectural overindulgence. At the southern entrance to the city, a towering orange ball with "76" in blue letters glowed like a neon hunter's moon.

On Easter Sunday, I slept well until the sun knifed through a gap in the curtains of my grandparents' trailer. Once I opened my eyes, I hummed with the energy of the road, wanting to get back on it and rack up the miles to Utah. I don't like anything to get between me and a drive, although I'll allow for a shower and a good breakfast as part of the ritual. The road isn't just a place and a drive isn't just a task. There's a connection to be made between driver and driven, and putting off the imminent encounter is like delaying the wedding night after the ceremony has taken place. Seven hours from Vegas to Ogden, but the journey wouldn't begin until one final hospital visit.

A day of hope and promise seemed out of place in that sepulcher. Good Friday fit much better. Death lingered like the acrid smell of urine. Grandpa was confused, unable to eat and wrapped in a wrinkled bag of bruised flesh. Dialysis treatments kept him alive, but each one plunged him into a state of restless, aimless determination. Again and again he struggled to rise from his bed, until the nurses strapped him to it. To his cross. A tepid bowl of broth was his sponge of vinegar, an oxygen tent his crown of thorns, a feeding tube in his side the thrust of a spear. I held his cold hand, patted his bony shoulder, and turned away.

Outside the room, a doctor told Grandma and me that Grandpa could do no better there than in a nursing home, or maybe even at home in the trailer park. I found that hard to believe. The grandpa who lived at home played exquisite chess, read ravenously, handled the guitar and mandolin as an accomplished musician, and loved long discussions about grammar. That grandpa had already died.

In thirty minutes I was back on the road, skimming past the surreal city. Soon the freeway led into a wide, flat landscape, as if Las Vegas had been a dream. Towering metal structures held sagging power lines that stretched into the distance. I looked into my rearview mirror and imagined what Lot's wife saw as the desert swallowed up the city. This would be more than just another drive home along a stretch I had traveled before. As much as I recognized the landscape, I knew it would not look the same. Nothing in the world would ever look the same after what I had seen in that hospital room. I thought Grandpa was the person most like me in the world, and I knew I probably flattered myself to think so. Besides chess and music, we shared writing. He had been a freelance writer for many years and had also written an outdoors column for a newspaper. I understood in that moment that he'd been waiting for me, watching my halting, uneven progress. And that I had been waiting for me. But I knew as I left Las Vegas that no breakthrough would happen in his lifetime. Guilt lurked in every shadow, regret in every crevice, the rocks and hillsides reminding my frail, transient self that the twisted Joshua trees would outlast me and in the end leave more of a mark on the landscape than anything I was likely to accomplish.

Now he was on the verge of leaving the land he had so enthusiastically embraced. And I could not save his knowledge or download his memories to a disk to be saved for future generations. As I drove, I looked for hope, for anything to give meaning to a world without the person whose knowledge and experience I so admired. I wondered if there was a way to honor him. Not by learning all he knew, but by learning all that I could know about the world around me. His collective landscape would soon fade into oblivion. Mine was just coming into focus.

Signs of promise appeared along the road: Pioche, Alamo, Caliente, the Great Basin Highway. Places I hadn't thought about before, out there somewhere at the end of a thread of asphalt that spun off from the freeway. Places that promised new experiences. I began to read each sign with wonder. "Entering Moapa Indian Reservation" and "Valley of Fire." "Ute, Exit 80, no services." I wondered who lived in Carp or Elgin or Hidden Valley, but not enough to take one of the exits. I wasn't ready to leave the freeway yet. It offered a panorama along with security. These were new feelings and I couldn't be rash. It was enough to see for the first time what I had only looked at before. To the north, furrowed foothills reached up to barren mountains, and the sharp contrast of sun and earth made a mural of the horizon.

An aluminum box of a motor home lugging in the lane ahead broke my concentration. Its Alberta license plate proclaimed VEGNOUT, and a sixtyish couple sat in its captain's seats. I tried to picture myself at that age, driving across the country. I couldn't imagine how I would look, but I could feel the pleasure of driving without a deadline into the landscape that lay before me.

I held that thought for miles, wondering if after all those years I would be merely enjoying the landscape or still searching it for answers. A flashing electric billboard interrupted my philosophizing. It popped up unexpectedly on the horizon as the road twisted in the direction of a mountain range looming ahead. Plastic bumps along the center line thumped their staccato warning that my tires were straying over their paved boundary. A small sign along the road told me what I already knew: that this was Mesquite, Nevada, a tiny border town invisible behind two large casinos. At about the same time, a strong, earthy smell filled my nostrils. On the right side of the road, cattle wandered within the fence of a feedlot. A casino peeked over the hill behind it. A harmonic triangulation of desert, ranching, and gambling that had escaped me before, when all I noticed about the place was that I could stop for a bathroom break and pull a slot machine handle or two on the way out.

The road wound off into more sagebrush and toward another road sign: "Arizona Welcomes You." I eased off the gas pedal and conducted a mental search for the map that lay somewhere in the car. Arizona just didn't seem right at that juncture, and it never had. How could I be driving north and end up in Arizona? I'd always meant to look carefully at the map when I got home and always forgot. As I peered ahead, I remembered why. A solid chain of foreboding mountains cut straight across the direction I was driving. They surprised and awed me every time, and on this occasion they brought a bit of worry. How, I wondered, do I get through them? How did I ever get through them? They loomed, much more solid than my memory of having reached them, as if I had only crossed them in dreams, woken up on the other side.

This time I paid attention, searching the landscape for which way the road would go, trying to find an opening in the dark range ahead. All I could see was a thin line leading right up to the base of the mountains and disappearing. From where I was, it dipped and wound as if I would drive off the edge of the earth before reaching safe passage. I clung to this trail to oblivion. Exposed veins of rock slanted toward the sky in a massive defiance of gravity. A strong wind buffeted the car and whistled through the closed windows. I gripped the steering wheel tighter and squinted to read the small sign approaching on my right. "Entering Virgin River Gorge."

"Gorge" had never before sounded so foreboding. So severe. Somewhere beyond canyon, just short of abyss. Towering slabs of stone parted as I made a looping right. The rugged cliffs rose higher, beyond my line of sight as the road dropped deeper into the gorge's confines. I marveled at how sheer and rugged the land appeared in this crack in the world. Possessed by the immediacy of the moment, and unwilling to break its spell, I kept driving while fumbling for a notebook and pen. I was filled with the urge to pour words onto paper as they came to me, as if I were transcribing the images around me into text. With my left hand on the wheel, I used the right to scrawl on pages.

About a mile in, towers of stone rose out of the dust. The curves of the road mimicked a ribbon of muddy water off to the right. Then more open space appeared, letting in the sky. High above, white bluffs jutted out from the rounded hilltops, standing watch over the landscape. I had seen the rocks there before, but this time they seemed immeasurably old, as if they were shelves that held history aloft from human interference.

Finally, the gorge receded as the hills and rock gradually settled back into the familiar brush-pocked landscape. Miles off to the right appeared alien outlines of massive and geometric rock formations. The distant glimpse into Zion National Park reminded me of how much territory remained unexplored in my life. Territory I had always been content to see from a distance.

The road would bring me no closer to the park's boundary, but as its image faded behind me I knew that someday I would have to go back to explore. I needed to live by descending into the canyons, not by peeking over their rims. My grandpa's eyes were about to close forever, and I had fixated on the thought that all he had seen would be lost. But I realized on the road that day that all he had seen, and more, was still there, waiting for me.

I could see it all, and then I forgot. The notebook, shuffled further from my awareness as the weeks passed, ended up in a drawer full of half-conceived inspirations, the starts and stops of intention and distraction. I opened it only to put something in, and then I walked away.

Peninsula

OF ALL THE REACTIONS TO MY NEWS, delivered in the hallways, offices, and cubicles of the corporate office, one stood out as the most common.

"You're doing what?" he asked with the quizzical look I'd been getting all day.

"Going back to school," I said. "I just know that I need to write, and the best thing I can think of is to go to grad school. Become a master of the craft. I want to know what it's like to dedicate all my attention to writing."

I'd rehearsed those lines, or something like them, revising as I spoke them to new audiences.

"I really admire you," he said. "That takes a lot of courage. I wish I had the nerve to try something like that."

I smiled and thanked him. A glow of satisfaction and confidence lasted about five seconds. Then I considered the backstory. Inspired by successful therapy—for my doctor had declared it so—I meditated, contemplated, maybe even prayed, and a destination emerged from the noisy scrum of possibilities.

Lucidity? Enlightenment? Delusion?

No. Just Iowa.

My research had consisted of reading that Jane Smiley worked in the English department at Iowa State University. I hadn't read any of her work but she seemed famous. And I visited campus once. On a corporate trip to Denison, birthplace of fifties TV mom Donna Reed, I took a day to drive due east on Highway 30 to visit one of my sisters, who lived in Ames. While there, I passed through the campus.

The vast lawn of central campus, bordered by tall pines and heritage oaks, adjacent to small but compelling Lake Laverne, captured my imagination the way it has captivated prospective students for decades. The place was beautiful. "This," I said to myself, "is a university campus." I felt so with all deference to Pullman, with its hills and trees, an alpine island in the wheat fields, with the Moscow Mountains to the east. I had feasted visually on the Washington State campus for five years and always felt at home there. But something about Iowa State's open layout, the rolling park of central campus, the old architecture mixed with new—the sense of ease engendered by a landscape that did not feel flat but instead spacious—brought me peace. The moment gently nestled into my being.

Now I was drawn back to that pleasant memory. A move to the center motivated by my need to be centered. Untangling the snag of my life—a rat's nest of five-pound test filament sprawling out of a flip-bail fishing reel—would be as simple as snipping the line and starting over with what was left on the spool. I quit my corporate job, we sold our five-year-old house, and we headed to the Midwest. I had not the slightest concept of what I would write about, or in what genre, or to what end. Remarkably, I was supported in this venture. Conditionally.

The glassed-in press box at Jack Trice Stadium might as well have been a convection oven. I'd never liked August football games. Football should be played outdoors on a crisp day and watched under flannel and a sweatshirt. I sat at the end of one of the long, narrow press tables, my polo shirt already soaked. Moisture formed in my armpits as if I were leaking anxiety. Sweat ran down to my elbows, then dripped onto the floor. The profusion of perspiration embarrassed me in front of a group of people I didn't know.

I was living my part of the deal. I would earn a stipend and tuition waiver as a graduate teaching assistant, put in enough hours to hold a full-time menial job at the local newspaper while also writing a sports column, complete a thesis-option master's degree in English/creative writing, and do it all on schedule—within two years. That my wife quickly found a decent-paying and mildly rewarding job on campus did not change the terms.

On one of my first days in the department, I asked about Smiley and was told that she'd moved on. A little unnerved, I turned to another faculty member for some advice. She asked nicely, but with apparent skepticism, what I was doing there.

"To be honest, I'm not exactly sure how to describe it," I said. "I want to write about place, I think. Where we live and what it's like."

I felt a little sick. I'd sold my house, quit my job.

She suggested I write an essay along the lines of what I had attempted to describe. So I did, and returned a couple of days later for her to review it.

"You can write," she said. "But this essay has no direction. It's just descriptions."

I didn't know what to do about it, and I was still at a loss when I signed up for a class about environmental literature. There was such a thing? Yes, said Terry Tempest Williams, Barry Lopez, Gretel Ehrlich, and shelves of others. I read and listened, nudged from my isolation by their expressions of life lived in the landscape. I wrote a few paragraphs, took some tough criticism, and wrote a few more. It may have been weeks or months, but finally I realized that the landscape I'd been so happy to leave behind—the sage-steppe plateau—was still right there with me. Those dry, barren stretches were rich with memory and experience.

Most of Iowa was lived in my mind, imagining someplace else. At the beginning of my second year, I ensconced myself in the lower level of our house, tracing through memories of my years in southeastern Washington, poring over maps and photos spread across countertops in my writing space. Traversing experience and emotion through personal essays on a palette of landscape—the experience unfolded like a favorite blanket.

Even Hanford seeped its way back into my life. Looking for some extra part-time work over the summer, I wandered into a modest office at the Ames Laboratory on campus and was put to work producing information sheets about remediation work at the site. Radioactive waste that was never supposed to threaten groundwater was doing just that. A hundred-square-mile plume of contaminated groundwater contained four hundred times the amount of tritium allowed in drinking water. The head of this plume was 3.6 miles from the Columbia. Above and below the ground, miles of pipes snaked across the desert, carrying venomous radioactive slurry from one waste tank to another as part of the cleanup. But the slurry was often too thick to pump, clogging pipes and requiring a cleanup of the cleanup.

The official literature did not tell the story that would emerge and is still emerging. In 1942, the military regarded radioactive waste as an issue to worry about later. Victory demanded expedience. The problem is, later didn't come for about forty years. Buried underground at Hanford were 60 million gallons of radioactive waste in everything from stainless-steel containers to rusting barrels. More than 1 million gallons leaked. Waste in a few of the larger tanks produced hydrogen gas, raising the risk of explosion. Not all the threats were so well contained. From 1944 to 1971, 440 billion gallons of contaminated waste were simply dumped into the soil. Plutonium 239 has a half-life of 24,000 years. Iodine-129 has a half-life of 16 million years.

Some mistakes cannot be overcome within a lifetime.

We know about this only because we have opened our eyes and asked difficult questions. Scrutiny, like the incessant Tri-Cities wind, finally exposed the truth long hidden in the desert.

In desolation, concealment is a function of space, not cover. Sky is the only true high ground, and from there only the sun holds all in its glaring line of sight, witnessing what is invisible from distant perimeters. Below, the sandy soil gulps whatever is bequeathed to its care. Rain disappears as if it were a mirage; did it ever really land on the ground or did it simply vaporize as it approached? A puddle, if ever one forms, suffers a more ephemeral fate than the cloud from which it was born, sinking down into the soil as if aware of its own futility.

I debuted as a writer—not a sportswriter or a corporate communicator, but as a writer—at a conference in Kalamazoo. In a bland college classroom, I read an essay from my thesis, hastily revised under a willow tree just moments before the reading. Another writer, who was editing a journal, heard my work and invited me to submit. Those words ended up in a journal. A new world had been opened to me.

The local landscape eluded me in the blur of those two years. But I experienced moments: rich silence among the trees and in the halls at New Melleray Abbey; water gently lapping beneath Frank Lloyd Wright's Cedar Rock House; a hailstone just a bit smaller than a golf ball in the palm of my hand, cautiously fetched in the midst of a brief storm as one of its cousins shot past my ear before thunking against the turf. As rewarding as writing felt, those ephemeral encounters caused me to wonder if I was living the rest of my life out of line with my nature.

As I walked across campus for my interview, the only advantage I could imagine having was my familiarity with campus. Except that I had no idea where to find Marston Hall.

The job was in engineering communications at the university. I knew nothing about engineering. But the classified ad drew my attention as one of the few opportunities to work in Ames. Because the stopover for my dream had become home. We weren't going anywhere.

I hoped the interview would go better than one in Des Moines a few weeks earlier. The creative department of an ad agency had placed an edgy call for someone who could produce transcendent prose while contributing to the culture of the shop. I showed up with carefully combed hair and a tie. They were all twenty years younger and a generation hipper.

"That cover letter you wrote, that was something else," said the manager who interviewed me. "We just wanted to meet the person who wrote it."

She spoke the truth. They had met me, and from that point that's all they wanted to do.

From my office window in Marston Hall, I fed peanuts to squirrels and chipmunks. Nothing else I could do in that office matched the tingle of holding out a peanut for a chipmunk and then, as it grasped the nut with its tiny paws, feeling a gentle tug—a physical connection with a creature that was essentially domesticated but that was engaged in survival and would return to its burrow with the memory of where it could retrieve food. I would return to my own home wishing that it had all occurred in the woods, not my office.

I also accepted a gig writing a weekly column for the newspaper, as a replacement for a prominent poet, whose lyrical pieces were not columns as much as they were meditations. I didn't try to imitate him. But after a few failed attempts at producing more newspaper-esque products, I decided to go with my instinct, writing about my impressions of a folksy diner or a Quaker gathering under the title "You Are Here." (The irony was completely lost on me.) I was learning that place mattered as more than just an address. Place could explain something about people. It was the lens through which I could see them, relate to them. And I could learn about myself. I wrote once about the drought plaguing Iowa. About the emotional torture of the hope for and promise of relief.

Ames started to feel like a favorite pair of jeans. Comfortable. An easy option. I had never felt that way in Utah, and yet I stayed in Utah for ten years—many more, I reasoned upon leaving, than should have been allowed. And yet I was taking familiar steps. We'd bought a four-level house with a koi pond. How domestic. Would it happen to me again? Would I stay someplace merely because I didn't know what else to do? Those questions began to haunt me. I'd earned my degree and published. But those facts did not fulfill me. Instead, I fell into a pool of lost possibility.

I sat in my office one day and watched a raven undermine my intentions to feed a squirrel that lived in a massive pine across the way. I'd been leaving corn out for the squirrel but the ravens always seemed to get there first. So I decided to outwit the birds by suspending a cob of dried corn from a string, tying the other end to a branch. A large raven landed, walked back and forth across where I'd tied the knot, and studied the situation. Its shiny black beak turned from side to side as it considered possibilities. Then it straddled the loop of string around the branch, stretched its head downward, and grabbed the string with its beak. The raven pulled the cob up a few inches, put one long-toed foot on the slack, then took hold again and pulled some more. In ten minutes, it feasted on its reward.

I wanted to be the raven.

☙

"Nothing will ever satisfy you," she said, and I couldn't argue. The world does not look like much in the dark, but it was the world in which I lived. Dull obstacles, unpredictable pits and trenches, monsters and fear of monsters. I had no answer for it, no light. I couldn't tell her we should stay or advocate that we go. As we sat in our family room, I possessed no will to resist the forces weighing me into the ground. She's the one who saw what was happening, who applied for a once-in-a-lifetime job in the Bay Area, who had the offer in hand. I fed chipmunks and watched birds. We sat across from each other in silence. The room darkened quickly. Rain began. Then torrents of rain. A flash—lightning before we realized it was lightning. A pause before we realized it was a pause. Whum! Fierce thunder. Its shock wave blew the metal window blinds inward. As they rattled to stillness, wind-driven rain bled through the window frame and coursed down the wall. Still, we said nothing.

A few weeks later, I sat on my sleeping bag in a bedroom while movers cleaned the place out. A couple of days later, on Thanksgiving, I sat there again, eating a turkey leg and mashed potatoes out of a Styrofoam container and thinking hard about whether I should stay. I had tasted the sweet nectar of change by gallivanting off to Iowa, and now I wanted more. But the anticipation of moving to a new place was muted by the stark reality of the cost: even small homes in California were listed in the half-million-dollar range. Buying would be impossible. During our trip to the Bay Area for her final interview, we felt lucky to have happened upon a small, old house on the east side of the freeway in a mixed San Mateo neighborhood. Rent: $3,000 per month. The first strains of resentment arose as I realized we would move to cramped, expensive quarters with traffic howling from the freeway only a long Frisbee toss away.

My road out of Iowa traced a frenzied trip through vast stretches of yearning—not mired in the domesticated, numbing miles of Nebraska farms and ranches, but crossing over the Rockies, the expanses of undeveloped Wyoming land, the vast and unpopulated Great Basin of Nevada, the snow-draped shoulders of Donner Pass. I stood in the snow there, regretting my pace—pressing to reach a destination while already missing the journey. I passed through landscapes in the way I had passed through places most of my adult life, a passive and transient sightseer on my way to the next ill-fated, life-changing choice. I did not want to leave. I did not want to arrive. I drove as if I were driven, wired with the blind belief and raw fear of a suicide bomber, awaiting my impact.

On the San Francisco side of the Bay Bridge, I missed the corkscrew exit to the 101.

"I don't know where the hell I am!" I yelled into my cell phone, driving along a city street with the look and disposition of a rabid dog. I yelled and yelled. I considered whipping the SUV around and driving straight back. I raged and pounded my fist and yelled some more. I hated the place before I spent a night there.

Riding my bike on a paved path along the bay near the San Mateo Bridge, I inhaled deeply at the long curve where a licorice whiff of fennel masked brine that smelled of decay. Discarded tires poked above the surface in the shallows of the near-lifeless inlet. A half-mile farther down, wind surfers plied the waves a hundred yards off a beach, no tires in sight. I had to admit there was a certain lure to a place that reminded me so much of Seattle. Those bike rides, and glimpses of the Crystal Springs Reservoir in the midst of undeveloped tree-green patches along the I-280. And from my fourth-floor converted hospital room of an office, the hypnotic diurnal dance of the fog, its delicate tendrils teasing over the northern reaches of the Santa Cruz Mountains in advance of an impenetrable gray mystery.

As the weeks passed, I grasped and clawed at these moments, taunted by every sighting of a dot-com kid driving a Ferrari while I languished on choked freeways and stopped-up bridges in the delusional longing for an affordable home. Loathing arose all too easily from disgruntlement. These feelings were far deeper than the open distaste I had developed for Utah. I despised where I lived. I resented it. I wished ill for it. I drank to forget that I lived there and that I wrote newsletters for my share of a living. Even the dot-com bust poisoned my schadenfreude by decimating the only stocks I owned—gifts from my grandfather via the bounty of North Dakota—and in a short, sickening span of mere days during the collapse they went from a healthy chunk of money to a handful of hard crumbs.

I drifted deeper into my own fog, flailing in exasperation but finding nothing to hold on to. I wanted to change everything but did not have the courage to change anything. Somewhere in my chaotic mind, enough neurons found their way to one another to conspire on a course of desperate action: disintegration would be a change.

So I explored the delicious flavors of self-sabotage until the range of options finally narrowed to one: I would leave. I was done with trying, and she was done with me. We talked it through one final time. I would leave the next morning and not return.

As I blearily emerged into the living room after a fitful sleep, she uttered some matter-of-fact words to me from the kitchen. Check the TV, she said. Something's happening in New York City. Some kind of a plane crash. A building was burning. I watched the confusing story unfold, coffee mug in hand, ate a few bites of cereal, and watched more. She watched, too, from behind me or beside me, from whatever separate dimension she now occupied from me. Two people in the same room, ties severed but ties remaining, already numb from our own drama and watching this one in growing disbelief. Then the second airliner plunged into the second tower of the World Trade Center.

Implosion.

Twenty minutes on my eight-mile daily dose of the 101 passed quickly as I listened to news reports on the radio. An explosion at the Pentagon. Another plane missing. All on the day that I had chosen to plunge myself—or had the day chosen to plunge me—into the isolation of an unknowable future. At the hospital, which overlooked San Francisco International Airport, a large group of us convened in a conference room to review our emergency status. We were the designated triage center for any major disaster at SFO. As we talked, as the day transpired, as news releases were written and phone calls made, the catastrophe occupied my external awareness and masked the void carved by leaving home that morning. What kind of a world had I just entered?

At the end of the day, I headed out of town with a small collection of recently purchased camping equipment in the back of my Pathfinder. My new home. I would sleep in San Mateo County Memorial Park, in a campground sparsely populated by redwoods and late-fall campers. I arrived after sunset, carrying fresh images of carnage from the nonstop radio reports. At my site, reserved and paid for in advance, I stepped out into dark silence. Alone. Disconnected. Faced with myself, and myself alone, I made a dispirited attempt to set up a tent, my hands and feet slowed by syrupy uncertainty. Marauding raccoons smelled my hesitation, tugging at my gear on the ground, then, when I tried to shoo them away, pawing through the groceries in the back of my SUV. In defeat, I cleared them from the truck, climbed in, and pulled the hatch closed. Curled up in fear, swallowed by the profound darkness, I held my knees to my chest and slept.

Over the next few weeks, I unfolded into the place. There was time before my twenty-five-cent morning shower and after my evening commute—traversed on a forest road as twisted as a neglected garden hose—to absorb the sights and sounds of my surroundings. The persistent squawking of demanding Steller's jays and the low, lazy bugle of unseen ravens. The muted click-clack of claws as gray squirrels weightlessly scampered up the soft, thick bark of redwoods—trees that were neck-binding straight, dizzy tall, that had been there since forever, occasionally dropping golden branch tips or green seed pods on the ground as shoulder taps to remind me they were alive, maybe even aware. I shared this space with incessant raccoons, scheming and resourceful in their quest for every scrap of available food, and a casual skunk that would wander past my tent each evening. Only once did I see a deer, a sleek four-point munching on roots next to a dusty trail on Pescadero Creek. I flattered myself when I got within twenty paces undetected. Then he looked up, his measured confidence aimed straight at me, and returned to foraging.

While I bristled at the prospect of other campers next to me, I welcomed the presence of the scattered few that occupied sites a few hundred yards away. As much as I embraced this small realm of quiet and calm, I could not have endured ten minutes of being entirely alone there, fearing the mayhem the darkness would have wrought. I drank a six-pack in half an hour by the campfire one night, then drove into town the next morning dirty, smoky, half-crazed with hangover, for an appointment I'd made. Some professional help was in order, I figured. Maybe stopping all my meds hadn't been a good idea. But when I walked into the wood-paneled office, I could sense a mistake. Mine or someone else's. The psychiatrist, dressed in an expensive suit and elevated by an air of elite ability, listened patiently as I strung together a stream-of-consciousness account of the previous months.

"I'm afraid there's been some misunderstanding," he finally said. "I don't see patients on a referral basis."

Yes, I could tell I did not belong.

"But before you go, I want to tell you something." He leaned forward, and I was going to believe whatever he said. "That brain of yours," he wagged a finger, "that brain of yours is going to lead you to spectacular success, or it is going to be your undoing."

I considered his words on my way back to the campground. One. Or the other. Could I find no place between? In the meantime, more mundane decisions awaited. According to the campground rules, I could stay only so long before having to move on.

So I searched for a new place to pitch my tent within a reasonable drive to work, and I found it at Half Moon Bay State Park. I had been to the general location a few times in the previous months, since it was the most direct way to get from San Mateo to the Pacific Ocean. The short, hilly drive through thick growths of eucalyptus took twenty minutes when traffic was light, but was akin to a ten-mile-long line at a fast food drive-up window during commute times and on the weekends. Such prohibitive traffic contributed to my resentment of California. As a nearly native Washington State east-sider, I had dreamed all my life of living near the ocean. Pines and mountains moved my spirit, but the ocean—the ocean made me swoon. As fixed in my mind and spirit as the salt air in Seattle was a family vacation to the Olympic Peninsula and Washington coast. We stopped in Long Beach, where I learned about clam guns, and drove through La Push and Neah Bay, where the sand in the washing machine at a Laundromat filled our clothes with the tawny grit we'd hoped to shed after accumulating it on the beach. Those small peninsula towns and the stony shores they occupied called to me as if they'd been my home from a time I could not remember. That sense of familiarity and comfort never left me.

I would return to the ocean when I could to be re-baptized into the faith that life was worth preserving, if only for those serene moments. But my dream of living near it had faded as I came to understand the barriers of expense and population, with the turning point coming on the day that I read that 50 percent of the US population lived within fifty miles of the ocean. Even the ocean's lure couldn't draw me into the masses, and I would never be able to afford exclusivity or isolation.

So from San Mateo, Half Moon Bay might as well have been on the other side of the Cascades. Even as I selected and paid for the patch of sand on which I would pitch my small tent, I understood that once again this would be a temporary arrangement, and that most of the time the tent would be empty while I was in my office. As the October days grew shorter, I left each morning in the dark, showering in the workout room at the hospital and dressing in my office, and by the time I returned, only a brief period of daylight remained for me to gaze out across the blue expanse. I sat and watched until there was no daylight at all. In the luminescence of moonlit fog, the white crests of inbound waves slashed across the surface like lit fuses as the surf tore and pounded at itself. Yet as the temperature dropped, my experience of the ocean took place from within my tent, where I shivered deep in my sleeping bag with a stocking cap on my head, listening to the rhythmic mantra of riptide and wishing for sleep.

The park, I discovered, was a must-stop for the steady stream of tourists and wanderers who traversed Highway 1. Each night, the occupants of million-dollar motor homes, the collections of pot-smoking backpackers, and those of us somewhere between settled into this ever-changing, eclectic community. In the brief pauses between crashing waves, voices and music tangled like competing cocktail parties. I wondered how it would be to just keep moving, to be part of the stream meandering from place to place. But I understood, from within the dark folds of my sleeping bag, that I would never be more a part of any of these groups than I was at that very moment, and that I could no more travel in isolation than remain in it. As someone who had tasted serious writing, who had failed in relationships and was failing yet again to find any fulfillment in respectable employment—who had turned to drinking too much too often, drifting back into and then out of counseling and therapy but steadfastly refusing more meds—I seriously wondered if self-destructive obscurity was my fate. I wondered if I could live like Bukowski, whom I had begun to read while still in Iowa, and read more after a visit to Lighthouse Books in the city. But I was coherent enough to fully understand that such a life came with a heavy price.

I wanted to live that way but I guessed that I could not. True, my life needed to be lived on different terms, but not those terms. I was ready to let go of expectations but still driven enough to seek my purpose. I still believed something else awaited me.

Something, or someone.

Like a moment of clarity that delicately dawns on a long, meditative walk, Grace appeared. We had known one another from work but the way in which we truly got to know each other said much for the relationship we would build. We walked. On a paved pathway in a narrow park along the bay. Among the trees on the hospital grounds. In the midst of massive redwoods at Muir Woods National Monument. We walked and talked, gazed at the clouds and the water, and mutually appreciated the subtle pleasures of beauty in nature and meaning in conversation. One late afternoon at the Pulgas Water Temple, as we watched the intricate dance of incoming fog overhead while I spoke of Iowa crows blanketing trees in their fall roost ritual, we understood something that at a conscious level would take many more months to emerge. We were at that place at that time, singular in our surrender to the moment, because it could be no other way.

Grapevine

IN THE WINTER OF 2001, I approached Santa Clarita Valley for the first time. I was skeptical. How could any place so close to LA become my next home? Had I not just resolved to flee the Bay Area, its breathtaking beauty choked by the dot-com kudzu of prices and people?

With a firm grip on the oversized wheel, I coaxed a U-Haul loaded with the detritus of my material life, Grace's car in tow. The rented truck's "check engine" light flashed and flashed as she followed in my Pathfinder—a caravan of faith in what might be.

My most immediate worry at that moment was navigating those twisting, steep curves in a steady rain with darkness impending, balancing an unwieldy load while watching the rearview mirror. I kept my focus on Grace while my past receded behind the mountains.

I thirsted for the tonic of an unknown and unexpected landscape. I did not know about the Tehachapi Mountains. About the climb as steep as a 737 takeoff, and the cool air, and the looming heights. My notions about the sprawling expanse of pavement and people known as LA did not include the deep, shadowy canyons carved like the grooves in elaborate woodwork along the southward edges of the Grapevine. My spirit rose with the ascent, swirled through the peaks around Pyramid Lake, and settled gently into the folds of the Santa Clarita Valley. In the shadow of Magic Mountain, in the safety of foothills folded like the sun-tanned forearms of a tough cop, I saw possibility.

We would live separately but together. She would finish her inter-rupted MFA, and I would stay out of her way. Support her. Be with her as we explored the idea of a relationship. We would occupy our own apartments and make no assumptions. To make enough money to live, I'd arranged work as an adjunct at a community college and would put in some hours at the local Barnes & Noble. I rationalized all this as a do-over. This time, I would devote my time to words—teaching, writing, working among them—without all the domestic demands and distractions. Iowa State had been an experience well intended but poorly executed.

The unbroken stretches of chaparral and sagebrush ringing a scenic valley north of Los Angeles lay before me like an unwritten essay. The drab green growth rooted to parched soil prompted me to find a deeper meaning in such an arid place. There was some-thing beneath the surface of this scabland. The rough tangle of heat-bent branches offered solace: a place to hide, to heal under a searing sky. The land held the seeds of an essay of hope.

In the spring, I circled back to explore what lay beneath my earlier experience with the desert. Not from a basement enclave. This called for a pilgrimage to fulfill my role as a writer and a seeker. So I flew to the Tri-Cities, stayed at my parents' house, and made arrangements to venture into the depths of my memories. My mother would drive while I sat with a notebook in hand, ready to transcribe what the place would speak.

We followed the gray, northward path of Highway 240 through the heart of the Hanford Nuclear Reservation. I gazed up at fat cumulous clouds; I imagined a lumpy, old comforter. Yet instead of drifting into dreams and half-slumbers on the cool April day, I drove deeper into my consciousness of the place.

I tried to remember how long it had been since I had traveled that road. Twenty years? Maybe I had never gone that deep into the forbidden zone of my childhood. Along the way, images arose in my mind as if I were recalling the episodes of a long-forgotten dream. Hills and fields seemed to be where I remembered them, but they weren't the same. Time had bent perception inward. The universe of my desert home was contracting before my eyes as houses and strip malls absorbed the open land around them and closed up the empty space.

As the miles accumulated and the city finally surrendered to country, I became even more disoriented. Among alternating circle-farm plots of plowed soil and young potato plants, the ground flowed with wavy, green cheat grass. This shouldn't be here, I told myself, yet it was, for miles in every direction. Where is my desert? I wondered. Where are my sand and my sagebrush?

The newspaper that morning proclaimed in giddy headlines that a record run of Chinook salmon would soon be churning through the local waters. The Columbia, Yakima, and Snake Rivers had not seen the likes of this for thirty years or more. Had I missed something? Had I not already mourned the impending extinction of such possibility? Within an article advising how and where to fish, for fishing would of course be allowed, came the admonition to keep only those fish with a missing dorsal fin—the indelible mark of a hatchery origin.

Chinook from a hatchery. Those fish were gods when I was a boy, glorious and unobtainable. Now they were swarms of planters.

Yet I could not deny the tingle when I looked down from the highway as we neared Horn Rapids, where a frail wooden platform extended like a half-hearted handshake into the rushing water of the Yakima River. No one stood there. Thirty years before, the platforms were as tightly packed as an urban business district, where Yakama Indians gathered to dip long-handled nets into the water to extract writhing silver salmon from the cold current. If I stopped and waited until dusk, when the salmon would be more visible in the water, would I see a fisherman with a dip net? Would he be as real as the images I had carried with me for so many years?

$$\mathcal{2}$$

They were images now informed by study; I'd learned more about the place as I learned how to write about it. So I could add this to my picture of the landscape: that around eleven thousand years before, a native inhabitant of the Columbia Plateau polished off a meal of fresh salmon and considered the rising wind slipping through the sagebrush, judging whether it was of the day-to-day variety or the precursor to a dust storm. Home likely was a rock shelter or cave along the Columbia. That centuries later, Native Americans crossed the barren plateau in search of food and trade, well ahead of Lewis and Clark. That within the next fifty years, their population was decimated.

There were other ghosts in that place. On the other side of the road, I caught my first glimpse of a sage skeleton, isolated and pathetic, as if it had died while reaching upward for help that wasn't there. We pulled off to the shoulder of the highway, and I walked out to the remains. Blackened layers of paper-thin bark covered the stiff branches. Damp and scored, it smelled of death, rooted to a bed of wet, cool sand. I stood and looked around. One by one, the other skeletons appeared as I learned to recognize death. I wondered if this was the scene of a skirmish or all that was left of the front lines of the fire.

Eighteen months earlier, a truck and a car collided and in three days, more than 160,000 acres burned. The first night, I read, crowds gathered on distant hilltops to watch the fire in the desert. Tendrils of flame raced ahead of the main body, fueled by uneven gatherings of sage and bunch grass, pushed forward by wind. Whirling flames coiled skyward and struck like rattlesnakes at the tinder-dry flesh of the desert. A plume of smoke rose fifteen thousand feet and flattened against the stratosphere, as if the place that had wrought weapons of mass destruction now lay prostrate before the shadow of its legacy.

Only a month before that event, nearly 50,000 acres burned at Los Alamos. Was this atomic karma at work? If so, Hanford paid a dearer price for its transgressions. Much of what burned was part of the Arid Lands Ecology Reserve—77,000 acres of land alongside Hanford, sequestered as a buffer zone to the secret go-ings-on within. Only days before the fire, President Clinton had proclaimed it and a fifty-one-mile stretch of the Columbia River as Hanford Reach National Monument—195,000 acres in all, look-ing much as it had before the arrival of modern civilization.

Over three days, flames leaped and swept over much of the mon-ument, yet they moved so quickly across the desert that pockets of grass and sage went untouched. At Horn Rapids Park, where the fire had jumped across the highway, I got out of the car again for a closer look at an area missed by the flames. Next to a small parking lot, buildings for restrooms were under construction and stacks of sod lay nearby. A gazebo had been erected at the be-ginning of an asphalt path that wound through clumps of sage toward the river. Murals depicted the local flora and fauna. My interest was in the Big Sagebrush, *Artemisia tridentata*. Just ahead, a few feet off the path, stood a specimen more than six feet high— large enough to be at least fifty years old. Sage looks scruffy and stiff from a distance, which is perhaps the image it must project to survive in such harsh surroundings, yet its thin, pale green leaves are feathery to the touch. Small waxy bulbs nest among the leaves that adorn the ends of straight, thin branches. Layered bark gives the branches a look of rolled-up newspaper. The scent of sage is subtle, even standing next to one, although its healing perfume filled my nostrils as I gently brought a branch to my face.

From what I had seen on the drive out, and from the results of the fire, sage was in trouble. Within steps of the six-foot sage that I stopped to visit was a six-inch sprout, lost among the cheat grass.

Without the benefit of stiff branches and facing so much competition from invading flora, it seemed too fragile to survive. Once the big sage next to me surrendered to the soil, would this one be here to fulfill the mural's depiction? I turned to touch its parent, as I imagined it to be, once more before I left, knowing that the six-footer survived in that fixed place for as long as I had journeyed in my peripatetic life. For it had witnessed the Yakama fishermen netting runs of native salmon from ramshackle platforms. It flourished through the phases of sage's life in the vicinity of atom splitting and plutonium purifying. Now it continued to thrive in the aftermath of wildfire.

Back on Highway 240, we drove away from Horn Rapids through fields of cheat grass, into the part of Hanford where the atom still makes its last stand. Off to the right I saw the 300 Area. It looked like an abandoned movie set populated by a gray dome, concrete smoke stacks, and aging metal water towers. Signs warned of radioactive waste nearby. The four-lane highway heightened the sense of isolation—there were no other vehicles in either direction on the long, flat stretch flanked by Rattlesnake Mountain and the White Bluffs above the Columbia. On the horizon, the oblong white dome of Fast Flux Test Facility revealed itself as would a full moon on a crisp spring evening. The road rose and the dome grew larger. On the other side of the highway, an alter-moon, gray and cold, more like an orb of Jupiter, rose from the desert floor. Its concrete surface looked fresh and new after the morning's rain. We turned down a side road and drove toward it, unimpeded. This place used to be forbidden to the public and now was foreboding only in its massive emptiness, like an unfinished mansion begun by an eccentric millionaire and abandoned to futility. As we pulled onto the gravel shoulder to turn around, I saw a sign that read, "If you hear a high-pitched siren, you have three minutes to leave the area." I scanned the landscape and wondered what exactly would be purchased by those three minutes. A final prayer, perhaps. Although no threat emanated from the vacant, incomplete reactor, the message carried meaning a few hundred yards down the road, where plumes of steam poured from the box-shaped confines of the Columbia Generating Station.

As we turned to drive back out of Hanford, I wondered if the healing power of the sage smudge was somehow brought into effect during the fire. Had the fire in the desert achieved any ritual success? The ashes of sage had given way to a soft covering of grass that would inevitably turn brown and be susceptible to another fire. The sheen of spring seemed as deceptive as the promises that the tanks and basins of Hanford would be finessed by the birth of new technology.

Maybe it didn't matter. Maybe my unchanging desert had already changed forever. The shrub-steppe fixed in my mind had incrementally retreated over decades of development. Yet through it all I shielded the original desert—the desert of first impressions—from intrusion. I wondered if the place was really so empty or if the emptiness is something I always brought to the place.

Back in my southern California apartment, I paced from kitchen to living room. My primary piece of living room furniture was a weight bench. I lived in a papier-maché shell of a place where I could hear even the refrigerator door being opened upstairs. With classes to teach and books to sell, and Grace spending twelve hours a day or more on campus, after a few consecutive days of routine, the apartment could easily become a cell.

I grabbed a map and drove ten minutes to a place called Placerita Canyon. Another five minutes on a trail, and the only sound was a bombinating wasp in a dry-wash gully so quiet even the thought of a mountain lion pricked the ears. Fresh breezes born over the ocean swept softly down the slopes. Outcroppings of granite and schist radiated waves of warmth, the breath of the hillsides as they sighed before sleep.

Over the months, I made this my safe place. Yet I also learned that just over the next ridge to the north, Santa Clarita sat like a Monopoly game played full-scale at two thousand feet, with identical box houses and town homes and condos stacked in ridiculous proximity on every space that could be cleared enough to accommodate them. From the mouth of the canyon, I carefully scanned the periphery of town and willed myself to see only mountains and shadows of mountains, blue sky, furrows and gullies, juniper, sage, and gingko. A neat trick. If I were not so careful, the full onslaught of civilization invaded my view—massive metal towers strangling the sky with high-voltage lines; cell phone relay towers with the egos of monuments standing atop the highest peaks; subdivisions past, present, and future infiltrating the habitat. Enough nature remained so the city was still a subplot in a larger drama, but I feared that native soil, grass, trees, and creatures were already assuming roles as bit parts for the next act.

At the beginning of summer, I witnessed firsthand as a developer tore the heart out of my desert muse. One day she reclined there, a millennium of repose ready to offer, in the whisper of a dusty wind, her most delicate secrets. A day later, her ghost swirled aimlessly among the earthmovers, and the bulldozers, and the devastation.

I felt like a fool. A few dozen acres between Sierra Highway and Interstate 14 had outlasted thousands of other acres already smothered under houses and industrial parks, and I celebrated that rough patch each time I drove past it. So what, I tried to tell myself. So what if yet another hillside was being pulverized into memory? I was just an itinerant in a land of immigrants, in California not to settle nor to prosper but simply to prepare for my move out of California. Grace would finish grad school and we would leave. Or she would. Or I would. There was no reason to care about the place.

I started driving there every day to see that stretch trounced by hulking yellow earthmovers pacing incessantly back and forth across the "property," demarcated by a temporary fence of orange plastic. Within a week, all the ground cover was gone. The big Caterpillars clawed away all but the brown soil, and then carved roads and trenches. Trucks spewed water to keep the land from blowing away, then more machines bludgeoned what remained. Finally, after two weeks, a sign went up: "Coming Soon: Canyon Gate. A private, gated community."

"So," I muttered, "desecration has a name."

I witnessed the same sight again and again as the city surged outward with scorched-earth edges. A few remaining old-timers lamented the loss of the valley, but most of them simply left because the sight made them sick, or they had been lucky enough to find a place that was what Santa Clarita used to be. Missing in the LA suburban bedroom was the sense of outrage or disgust that I thought should come with the inexorable destruction of nature.

After a while, all I could see was the damage. And it looked back at me from the mirror. I began to see with more clarity what lay before me in my own life and how little I could do about decline. Coming to terms with mortality meant acceding to futility. I could learn to make peace with my fate, but nothing, it seemed, could save places like Santa Clarita.

One day, as I aimed away from the madness and drove in search of emptiness, a coyote ambled across the road one hundred yards ahead of me. I marveled as if I'd seen a ghost.

Maybe I had.

Five Minutes to Midnight

WE SAT ON THE FLOOR of our one-bedroom apartment in Newhall and stared at the dingy carpet.

"I have to believe," I said, "there's a place out there for us. Why shouldn't we believe that? Why shouldn't we believe we can work at decent jobs and live in a nice little house and have a good life together?"

During her thesis year, I had come to Grace's apartment to eat, or sleep, or watch the television in the workout room because neither of us could afford cable. Once she graduated, we decided to live together, so I moved in. The romantic life of letters brought us together under that roof, then slipped out the door. We bought gas and groceries with credit cards and waved the white flag of minimum payments.

"I don't know where that is," she said.

And that's all there was to say. So we sat there—a thirty-something recent MFA graduate and a forty-something part-time community college instructor, checking our schedules to see if our next shifts at the bookstore overlapped.

Over the weeks since her graduation, we'd been scanning the map and imagining the places that might be our salvation. Before I knew her, Grace had traveled to China, Europe, and South America. As a girl, she spent summers in Panama, where her mother was from. So I imagined that with her new credential, we'd be off to someplace far away. A new life, a new adventure.

But it wasn't working out that way. Neither was the writing life. I'd started to fill new notebooks but didn't get far. Grading piles of essays and working part-time for minimum wage turned out to be a time-consuming exercise in financial futility. The books on the shelf at the store called to me, but I had no answers.

So I called in a favor, or called in and begged. My former corporate boss in Utah remembered me well enough to suggest a position at a Job Corps center in Massachusetts. They flew me out for an interview, and Grace arrived a couple of days later. I said what I needed to say, a spiritual tradeoff for mortal needs: medical benefits, a retirement account, a regular paycheck. We drove through Amherst, and to a park at the top of a hill, swooning at the splendor of a countryside in the midst of its fall transformation.

We returned to Newhall and talked for days about life in New England. The phone would ring at any time and we'd go. But it didn't.

I tried corporate again and received a new suggestion. After hanging up, I turned to Grace.

"So, what do you think of Reno?"

"We're not that desperate," she scoffed.

But we were. Days later, we drove there, stopping along the way to contemplate the otherworldly weirdness of the tufa at Mono Lake, and I interviewed. Shortly after our return, the phone rang. Grace stood at my side. I was offered a job at $32,000 a year.

"I have a job," I said. "In Reno."

We held each other and cried.

The voice from the radio said a winter storm was on its way. A big one. I was at the U-Haul store, checking out truck availability, so I called Grace.

"How soon can we be ready?"

"Well, now, I guess," she said. We didn't have much anyway. So I rented a truck and a trailer, and we spent the rest of the afternoon in frantic escape, hungry for refuge and that first full paycheck.

Just after midnight, we reached Donner Pass. The first wave of the storm had already hit and moved on. A single pathway of passable road remained open down the middle of the two-lane freeway, the headlights of the U-Haul gobbling up the white dotted line. Grace followed me in the Pathfinder. Fresh snow sparkled under a full moon. I could have fallen into the dream of our arrival on the Grapevine, but the truck's heater didn't work. I shivered and drove.

We arrived in Reno a couple of hours before daylight and checked into a cheap room for warmth and shelter until the office opened at our new apartment. The next wave of the storm moved in as I unloaded the truck, with Grace unpacking and organizing in the apartment. We finished as the brunt arrived, satisfied to watch the snow and unaware how our frantic two-step had just set the tone for the next ten years of our lives.

After declaring we were in Reno to get well, we began the process in our apartment next to a housing development rising from the sage. We kept taking the long walks that had defined the origins of our relationship, but now on paved pathways through the unfinished development. Mountain cottontails that lived in a littered wash hopped across and along the path; yellow-headed blackbirds squawked their rusty-gate calls from the reeds of a small pond shared with mallards and gulls. We wanted to be where there was more of all of this and less of all of us—the recently arrived émigrés filling every spare quarter-acre lot and two-bedroom, vaulted-ceilinged apartment that builders and speculators could contrive.

Then we discovered Cold Springs, a secret that had been well kept from us. Grace and I needed a map on our first trip there though we lived just twelve miles south. The last valley in Nevada on Highway 395 North comes into view with the subtlety of a girl who has inevitably—but unexpectedly, it always seems—become a woman. Only on the far descent of Granite Peak does Cold Springs Valley advance shyly from the shadows of the Diamond Mountains. As the highway dips and turns to greet her, the grassy alpine pastures of Heinz Ranch unfurl in easy waves that lap at the White Lake playa—sand so white that in the dusk it is truly a lake to the unschooled eye, reflecting the sky like a memory of its youth.

As if we were pushing a cart through the aisles of a big-box department store, we navigated streets as fresh as the map on which they were printed. Where self-imposed exiles once fled to live in manufactured homes among the coyotes and range cattle, a community had begun to grow phase by phase. We had wanted a house away from the city and with land around it, but the influx of California house-rich refugees had driven prices too high. Even in this place, on our way out of the main office, we heard one of them say, "We'll take two" with the casual tone of a shopper picking up a couple of melons at a farmers market.

So we staked out claim in the midst of the gold rush, choosing a 1,550-square-foot, two-story, half-framed structure at the end of a cul de sac. The tops of mountains, rising above the rooftops, filled the horizon from each window. Out of guilt and respect, we planted sage on a burial-mound berm in our xeriscaped front yard. Two plants to atone for the dozens that must have been plowed to make way for our suburban footprint. We lamented news of the impending doom of the ranch and of Reno's strategic annexations, and we spoke of where we might go, and when, because we could not bear to watch the destruction.

At least, Cold Springs offered landscape and a view of hillsides, not hillside homes. From there, just forty minutes to the northwest, we could camp and fish and hike among lakes and pine trees.

So when we bought, we did so with the naiveté of children, pretending that the half-built village would simply stop in time. We walked two blocks north from our front door beyond the edge of the houses and into the sage, like ghosts into our field of high-desert dreams. There, we took deep breaths and tried to memorize the view and, after one fresh snow, paced off the longest leap of a monstrous jackrabbit that had flown across our path. We walked and pretended, and spoke of the place as we spoke of our love for one another: beautiful, fragile, and well worth the journey. Even after the developers bulldozed the sage for a thousand more houses, we walked. Even after they laid the foundations, even after they began to pave the streets, even after they built some of the houses and people began moving in. Love is said to be blind, and hope is often best cultivated with eyes closed.

We chose Alaska for our honeymoon trip, wanting to experience a place new to both of us and free, or at least apart, from the housing boom we lived amidst. What we saw there was nature just being nature. The dull emerald waters of the Susitna River braiding through a rocky bed among the black spruce and birch, powering onward with the urgency of a spawning salmon, unmindful of a purpose yet fixed solely on its reason for being. Ironically, those waters—so forceful and so vital—were nearly void of life, being too full of glacial silt to allow it. Yet if we disappeared and the train carrying us north disappeared and all humans who could ever see the river disappeared, the Susitna would surge ahead with a more honest life than most of us could ever dream of living.

The river, the trees, the mountains, the earth, the snow—all functioning flawlessly in elegant symbiosis with the purest of motivations: simply being. Yet as the train from Anchorage to Denali followed the course of the river, I had to wonder if our being there, along with the three vociferous couples from Philly and the unimpressed world-traveling tourists from Denver and the distracted young family from Washington, and the hundreds of others on that train and other trains, somehow influenced the experiment. Did the observers affect the observed, even just passing by? Would the expanse from our windows truly be left to itself, or was there an uncertainty principle of landscape at work, ensuring that what we saw would never be the same simply because we saw it.

At the entrance to Denali, where ubiquitous construction and the beeping of bulldozers backing up for another run dominated the ambient wilderness sounds, I felt a surge of Cold Springs guilt. We could escape to the edge of the wilderness but not without the incursion of development on our heels.

Time and space advanced on Cold Springs Valley as methodically as a calculation. What had been a refuge from the city found itself on the event horizon of land-hungry Reno. The daily inspiration of those who lived there was threatened with 13 million square feet of industrial and business development and a thousand more homes. Acrid rumors of a Wal-Mart filtered into the air like smoke from fire smoldering over the horizon.

We received a mailer that contained details about the Cold Springs Collaborative Plan Effort. A "Subject/Task" draft schedule and gridline map reduced our country living aspirations to a series of strategic steps that would carve up the valley from stem to stern. A narrow strip of land snaking over our eastern hills would be the route of Reno's incursion: just enough of a corridor to connect the unbuilt half of our development to the city for annexation. Once accomplished, this step would allow the developer to build houses closer together, maximizing the payoff of every precious acre from us to the northern boundary of the valley.

We were beginning to think we helped to kill the place. What had we done? What could we do? We searched for answers, and each time we crested Granite Peak on our way home, we said our silent version of a prayer for forgiveness to the valley.

Before the housing boom, and even for some time after, Cold Springs Valley had basked in anonymity. Insulated from the city by Sun Valley, Panther Valley, Lemmon Valley, and Golden Valley, by Stead and Red Rock, Cold Springs lay one hill farther than most Renoites cared to venture. We often heard a delivery person or houseguest from Reno comment, "I didn't even know this place existed."

The well-defined valley rests among four ranges of hills and mountains. To the southwest and west, the grassy fields of Heinz Ranch rise into the scattered stands of pine that mark the benches of the Bald Mountain Range and constitute the fringes of Humbolt-Toiyabee National Forest. The Granite Hills, at 5,900 feet, enclose the eastern edge of the valley, which narrows to the northeast, ending in the hills of the Stateline Peak Mining District. Petersen Mountain, which runs its treeless north-south line to a peak of 7,800 feet, closes off the northern edge of the valley. Peavine Peak fills the horizon to the south. And in the middle, White Lake Playa, usually dry by May but still sheltering a sheen of water on its northern flank during a drought-breaking June, dominates the valley floor.

Just north of the playa was the half-circle of finished homes in the Woodland Village development; the other half of the circle was bare ground, the sage having been plowed. The valley's aspect changed with the light, the weather, and the season, offering a new perspective at nearly every viewing. Each drive home brought anticipation of how the valley would appear. The playa may seem like a deep alpine lake, or a desolate stretch of Sahara sand, or a mirage of waves shimmering like mercury in motion. The hillsides may appear coffee brown, or sage green, or as a mixture of red, yellow, and ochre hues, with morning or evening shadows etching ever-changing woodcut patterns for dramatic effect. Cloud cover may draw the valley floor higher, or deep blue skies inspire a breathless descent into the valley's midst.

On our way back home from a shopping trip late one afternoon, Grace and I witnessed a vision in that place. In the low-angle light of June dusk, after hours of easy, steady rain, a laser-bright sunburst engulfed the entire western edge of the valley. Mist rising from the mountains glowed as if a star were being born in their folds. We gazed and gasped, and as the highway bent north we witnessed the portals through which we had passed: two rainbows, side by side. We were so small, and the glory around us so immense, that the universe could not have been bigger than what surrounded us in that moment. In another age, the scene would have inspired a legend that seekers of truth would have devoted lifetimes to pursue. The moment was an ephemeral slice of timelessness, a single deep sigh in the midst of a day contorted by the stressful spasms of modern life.

Grace turned to me and asked, "Is this heaven?"

"If there is such a place," I replied, "it had better look like this."

We spoke wistfully of why we should always carry a camera, and I wondered: If we lived here the rest of our lives, would we see this again? Would the sunburst and the rainbows and the mist ever return in exactly that way? Would it matter if below them were the roofs of warehouses and parking lots, as long as we could look up and see nothing but beauty?

But that was the point. We didn't want to have to look up. We were searching for the fairy tale—that place where time is measured by the girth of a tree, where the only necessity is an awareness of the moment, and where the rhythm of flowing water whispers "you are safe here, safe," each fluid pulse a mother's fingers running through her child's hair. This was the place that we wanted to call home.

After we arrived at our house, I looked out at the sage shrine in our front yard and saw dozens of tiny sage springing from between the rocks, spreading out from under the branches of their parents. They were alive with possibility.

Return

IN THE EVENING, AS WIND SWEPT down off the hills, free to wander as the sun turned its back on the day, I understood the source of the silence. The coyotes were gone, and had been for a while. Their melodic yip-yip-yips used to accompany the evening breeze, but now it was only the wind, blowing through vacant streets and wooden frames—the tangible intentions of progress.

Gunfire had stopped for the day. Somewhere out there, on the edge of the built world, the shooting pop-pop-popped intermittently from dawn to dusk. A walking path alongside our house—what we had imagined as a buffer between us and the neighbors—carried the ATVs and dirt bikes on their way out, riders with guns strapped to their sides and across their backs, fathers and sons armed for their day together.

I'd lost twenty dollars that afternoon because I lost the will to resist. The slots could find me even as I drove down the street, and usually I could talk as good a game as they could, shutting down their noisy clatter with a little reasoning or even outright rejection. Sometimes I accepted the dare. Twenty, I would say. Just twenty. And I'd walk away relieved that I'd gotten it back, or even most of it. A little hurt and angry if I let it go. Sick, if the machines, howling like hyenas, had taken more. I spat back at them that I was still to the good: our first week in Reno, I'd put a precious twenty into a machine when twenty was a day of food, and the reels lined up to surrender 480 dollars. Don't forget that, I would tell them. I've had the better of you.

This room I sat in, the breath of the hills fluttering through the blinds, was the same where I had once yelled at God, and really, I had meant it. Grace was out of town, and I'd lost my will to a bottle of Scotch. In fact, the topic that night was a review of my penchant for losing: losing my nerve in a classroom of Job Corps kids, with their quick streetwise discovery of me as easy prey; losing my dignity as an adjunct who couldn't break through at the community college; losing any sense at all of a direction as I lurched from job to job, still imagining a writer lay within the shell of teacher or editor or whatever else I was being paid to do for as long as I could stand to do it. So that night, sufficiently sorrowful for my own missteps and on the precipice of blind intoxication, I yelled upward, confident that was the right direction, "What do you want of me! Tell me! Tell me!" I cried, and thought for a moment of the moon over the beach at Lincoln City.

❧

The defining moment may have come when we passed one another on the divided highway, Grace driving home, me driving to work. Maybe our wistful waves to one another merely set our minds in motion. But the afternoon we visited the daycare center—then we knew.

"Here's the baby room," the girl said cheerily, and she was a girl, not yet a woman, despite her confidence. A few infants strapped into swings tick-tocked in the center of the stark room. "We make sure they get regular attention." Tick-tock, tick-tock.

"Nice," we lied simultaneously, coordinating our turn back to the door to avoid tripping over one another.

"I don't think I can do it," Grace said in the car on our way out.

"Oh, we definitely can't do it," I said.

When the doctor confirmed her pregnancy, we had celebrated with more than just a little satisfaction at our control over the situation. Through her character-defining attention to detail, her dog-eared book and folder of heavily annotated graph paper, and her fervent dedication to diet and abstinence from alcohol, Grace had willed us—she of "advanced maternal age" and me, simply old—to nearly immediate success. We were already painting the nursery, a bedroom near ours upstairs. She taught as full-time, tenure-track faculty at the community college, and I held a full-time job that wouldn't end just because the semester did.

But now this. What were we going to do about this?

For weeks we talked, calculated, and fretted. We painted and bought baby furniture. We talked, calculated, and fretted some more. There had to be a place, we reasoned, where we could be a family without all the driving and dropping off and wondering who was raising our child. Where schools were safe and good, and life could be lived in peace. Maybe even where Grace could choose to stay home and devote all her time to being a mom. But we owned a house and held full-time jobs. Where was this place, if it wasn't Reno?

Tick-tock.

Finally, I decided to ask. I still don't know why.

"What about Iowa?"

The realization wobbled my legs as I walked alongside Marston water tower, that silver, gangly relic of engineering history: I was in Ames, taking steps to return there as a home.

Our reasoning had gotten me here. This exercise was all about son-to-be and mother (now eight months along). She wanted to stay home with him. Everything had become about him: neighborhoods, schools, clean air and water, a house with character. All I understood about being a father was that I wanted it all for him. And for her.

Campus felt familiar, but not the refrain in my head. This coming back to a place was something I had never experienced before.

I sensed dissonance. Imbalance. My presence forced, alien. I stopped and stood still in the July sun, perspiration tickling under my shirt. Yes, I had become quite good at leaving. But returning would be difficult. Just as I was in the moment, maybe I simply needed to stand still.

So much of my life had been about movement and change. Would it be possible to stay in Iowa by really staying: same house, same relationship, same job. Could I really do it? Could the flow of life take place within these boundaries, rather than spilling out over the banks of place and relationship and source of income? Are they even the same kind of flow, these peregrinations and dramatic changes compared with deep explorations of house, family, job?

"I want to find out," I said aloud, still listening as a skeptic.

Later that day, after the interviews with mostly familiar people and tours of mostly familiar places, I looked out the hotel window at a sprawling lawn, the air hazy with humidity. There's only so much to see in the middle of Iowa, or so long-timers would have you believe. They talk about the landscape being too green after a wet spring—so green that the visible spectrum is swept over by every increment of green that the wavelengths will allow, even in the aura of the place: the subtle green glow of dusk appearing in a warm vase of clouds, delicate as a vague intent and gone into the fading light by the time conscious thought invades. But when the hothouse climate yields to crisp late-October air, green gives way to ascendant yellow and gold on the branches of sugar maples that glow like embers under a perigee moon.

There's only so much to see, but is there a reason to look for more?

Once back at our house in Nevada, we stood in a backyard covered with gravel, peering past the nearby street and over the multiplying rooftops, asking ourselves if not seeing the flanks of Peterson Mountain or Peavine Peak every day, watching their colors and shadows shift under the passing sun, would somehow be an unacceptable loss.

What she saw, exactly, I cannot know. Even as we stood hand in hand, wondering if the mountains had one last thing to show us, I did not know if she saw the same mountains as I did. For I saw a portal into a landscape of memories, of a patchwork life threaded by the road to the next place and filled by sights of what was out there, always out there, always beyond reach, but within the range of visibility.

Iowa is a place of sound footing, where the earth is for roots, for families. For generations. Filled with that spirit, Grace and I flipped through photos on a real-estate website.

"If you can find me a house on Ross Road, I'll move," she had challenged me. We knew of that street at the edge of Ames because it ran along a tree-filled park that matched our idyllic dreams.

We found the house and we bought it, sight unseen—except for the photos. One had been taken from within an oak-floored room with banks of windows overlooking the park. We accepted the promise of what might be seen from there, gazing into the future—of that vista, of life in a midwestern college town. We closed our eyes and we saw ourselves.

To get to work, I walked through the park and the trees, my daily commute a communal opportunity. Some days, distracted and tired, I merely walked. Some days, I stopped on a small wooden bridge. This day.

The mud and gravel bottom under the riffles of low-flowing College Creek isn't the channel merely for College Creek—it is the way of all flowing water, from the Columbia, Snake, and Yakima, to the Truckee, to the Susitna, to unnamed streams in the Cascades, to the little boy's playground of irrigation runoff in Kennewick. Water rises, sinks, swirls, roils, ripples, and churns through channels, oxbows, rapids, and dams. But most of all it flows, as it has always flowed. And as I cross this creek it is not simply a crossing; it is a confluence of that instant of flowing water with all my experience of flowing water, a resonance of moment with deep experience. And I realize that my crossing is not so well defined—that I have crossed the creek all the way to the creek, and that I will keep crossing long after it is behind me. The water follows its own channel and I follow mine, but something larger contains us both. We are separate only in the insistence of human self-absorption that we are separate. Defy that perception, and the water and I swirl along together with no thought of channel and no awareness of destination or purpose, only of movement.

In the darkness of my mind, a different universality reigns. This is a flat, gray world that can be traversed only by trudging. Please, let there be no unexpected glorious sunsets, no hint of an interesting destination, no thought of a dalliance off the beaten path—let there only be a tomorrow with more of the same despair, for it is safe and predictable. I know this world well. Perhaps, like the creek, I have never left it and am walking it today, somewhere in the background, as the path I follow cuts a scribbled trail like a black vein in my mind.

Did I choose correctly?

I have spent most of my life wondering who I am supposed to be—who or what I am meant to be. My destiny, perhaps. But I am haunted by this. Consumed. And just as I find that all places are but one place, I find that after decades of wandering and searching, even sometimes praying, I have no idea who I am supposed to become—and continue to be convinced that I am to become someone. As with place, I am the same, with the same questions, the same yearning to know.

Perhaps I live in the mind of a child. My life has been a little of this, a little of that, like the child who tap dances and plays piano and paints by the numbers only to become the adult who regards those dalliances of youth simply as part of growing up. Yet in my view of myself, and of the landscape, I am still the child. The landscape is but one more of my dabblings. I view it, I experience it, I write about it, I feel emotional attachment and pain and loss, but I do nothing more. I see it as a child sees it, irrationally wanting it to stay as it is, or to resist encroachment, or even better, to return to a magical unspoiled state. But my experience of the landscape is mostly in my mind.

Father, husband, worker. I spend so little time any more in that imaginary place, where I can leave myself open to what the landscape might tell me. Or I have stopped taking the time. Or I have finally stopped believing that the landscape can, or will, tell me anything at all. Whether the secret was always there or never there, I have not been able to discern it.

On a morning walk around Lake Laverne with my wife and son, the distant cumulous formations, baroque in gray and blue draped with garments of soft, angelic white, are that morning's clouds and no others, even though I have seen those dramatic views on so many mornings in so many places. And the little bluegill in the lake, pitter-pattering through the shallows like baby feet, are these bluegill; even though they may be some of thousands in this lake, another generation of seamless generations, and even though they incite flashes of memory, a bamboo pole in my hands on Big Lake or a bucket splashing with shiny, scaly sides on the alkali shores of a nameless Potholes pond, these bluegill are of this place and this moment. This feeling is distinct, the quarter-hour bells of the Campanile floating from beyond the trees on the far side of the lake—yes, they are of each quarter hour, but these bells on this lake at this moment are my experience right now, my son in his stroller searching for the cardinal singing from an overhanging tree branch, Grace leaning into me with her arms wrapped around my waist, and of all that has passed, love, sights, songs, of all that makes this scene what it is in all its fullness, there is still—separate, at its own altitude, as a crow soaring through a curve of whimsy— this very experience, ephemeral and beautiful.

This is the experience of singularity, and such moments stir feelings in a bittersweet mix of what is, what has been, and what may come, reminding me that the distinct moments are the ones that we build stories around, even if the lessons are universal.

Before my son was born he went on a hike across the faces of boulders—creased, gray faces peering up from the earth, the sagacity of eons in those brows. The rocks, and their timelessness beside foaming rapids, led my pregnant wife and me down a tricky slope to the rushing, swollen Yuba River. From inside his mother's womb, could our son hear the whoosh and sense the flow? Did he feel the connection of his mother's feet to the ancient rocks, of her hand to the cool ripples, of her mind to the wide blue sky? Could he know what we knew, that the moment was a cherished one of solitude and anticipation that we could only hope would find residence in our memories? Could he grasp at some level that his parents, who had finally found lasting love in a place of pine trees and fog and flowing water, were marking one year of marriage, and perhaps their final quiet time as Two, as close to the natural world as six months of pregnancy would allow?

Before my son was born, the clear, still water of Pyramid Lake lapped at his mother's belly on a late spring morning, Lahontan cutthroat slipping between the rocks just a few feet away, seeking a mouthful of minnow. Could he hear the whistle of a white pelican's wings as it glided inches above the surface for a landing? Did he grasp the calmness of his mother's gaze over a place still managing to evade the decay of progress that was despoiling its way across the Palomino Valley? Did he know as his parents knew that this would probably be the last time that they would be in this place in this way, and that if they were to return, that it would not be the same?

I consider all the change that I have seen and I lament. Most of what I have witnessed is decline—or, at least, what I regard as decline: open spaces being filled or altered in some other way that is not nature's course. I feel that way while fully understanding that my own presence has contributed to such change. Have I not, in every instance, lived in a place that was once natural landscape? Perhaps Reno was the turning point, as I witnessed the sagebrush being plowed and the high-desert contours being flattened to accommodate development after development, one of them containing my own home. Perhaps it is the cumulative effect of the country's population having grown by sixty million in my lifetime. I can feel it. And what I sense is that all the landscape I have seen and experienced, knowing all the ways that it has shaped me, is changing. All that I know is slipping away, just as I am slipping away into middle age and beyond.

The landscape that my son will become aware of, that will influence his life, will be all that he knows. Will it have the same effect on him that it did on me? Will he reflect and explore and probe those connections, or will he not share my perspective? And will it matter to him, what I have seen and what has shaped me? I wonder about the world in which my son will live, and if, when he gets to the age that those sorts of questions might come to mind, there will be any place I can take him to show him what made me who I am.

All that will be left, I'm afraid, are stories.

2

There is flat and there is flat. What some people regard as visual desolation is to me a landscape of opportunity. There is room to see. Anyone who thinks every field of corn is the same is simply not paying attention. Yes, it's easy to be lulled by uniformity of height and color, with the subtle differences of strain and genome undetectable to the eye of the nonfarmer; only the colorful lines of seed and pesticide signs suggest diversity. Evenly spaced rows of geometric integrity eventually swallow perception like the disappearing space between trees in the depths of a sprawling, thick forest. Maybe there is some flat land where corn by the thousands of acres blankets the landscape with disorienting solidity, but even there the fields are not the same. Not when seen in the low-angle light of dawn, the vernal slant of mid-morning, the shadowless scrutiny of midday, or the long wavelengths of sunset. And for even more effect, the fields of Iowa rest on rolling hills—these are not salt flats covered in corn. Even the subtlest nuances of topography are enough to reflect and absorb light in visually meaningful ways, to say nothing of chlorophyll content, plant height, the sun's angle; of cloud types or no clouds at all; of temperature and humidity; of the perception of the beholder at that or any moment.

Such details float through my mind on a Sunday drive along Highway 69, a two-lane stretch running next to I-35 and presenting a parallel world of farm houses, not fuel stops, and the chance to slow for a sublime scene or to appreciate that—in just the right light at just the right angle at just the right speed—rising and falling hills of corn or soybeans appear like waves in the ocean, copper-hued, pre-harvest waves of promise. But what I see is more abstract, the imprint of furrows and fields from my childhood trips now worn nearly smooth. And what Grace sees, I cannot know, but she's got one arm out the window, clicking away at a tightly clutched digital camera, and when she draws it back inside after we've passed an old white church pegged by a steeple into the middle of a vast field, she smiles under tousled hair and says, "God and corn."

I smile, too, and those are the only words for many, many miles. Our toddler son is asleep in his car seat and this is as close as we often get to quiet quality time. Time with a view. I wonder, as we drive, if what I have sought is still in the distance, or if the distance, like the time I see before me, has grown shorter. Maybe the lesson, in this land where mountains are a memory and the desert is the past, is not in what I can see out there; maybe I am at the place that I have always sought and I am just learning about how it looks to be there.

Landlocked Reality

WRITING ALWAYS BEGINS as a distant feeling that I am going to write, so the dream was no accident. In the dream I was reading a novel and paused at the end of a stirring passage, absorbed by a yearning to be able to write like that. Then a noise. The author had arrived at my house. He was there to move the large, jagged rocks scattered across my yard—a yard of dust and desolation—for a small payment. Money for food, he told me. I paused again, this time to question my yearning and to consider the true price of talent.

Today, I write. Needful writing. A primitive process that is more instinct than careful consideration, and even though I write about my experience, it is more dissociation than memory. I can see a two-car, two-career couple escaping Reno, where the high tide of California money and population had begun lapping over the top of the Sierra. They knew they were soon to be three and in their eyes was a longing for a place that was more like them, where the next sunset was more important than the next freeway expansion. Someplace centered and safely insulated from the frenetic, urban ideal.

They searched for their island.

In my basement, where I retreat to write, I fall into flashback because I am living in one. I am trying to layer a new experience over a familiar landscape littered with bittersweet memories. I am plowing this rocky field that once defeated me, yet left me yearning for more, certain that hard work and sincerity of purpose would pay off.

Grace stayed home to be with our son, who for four years witnessed the rhythm of nature in the animals and birds that stream through our yard from the park. We cautiously approached a snapping turtle in the grass across the street, and we marveled at the theater of fireflies on dark summer nights. The changing seasons pass through our picture windows like living wallpaper, the golden glow of fall enough to transport that room and everyone in it to a place like the one that is supposed to await the faithful.

These are dreams. But we must live our lives awake.

When floods swept through Ames in the midst of a brutal summer, after tornadic winds shredded and toppled sixty-foot trees in our backyard, after a crushing winter during which deer and rabbits ravaged our backyard hedges for survival, Grace and I sighed and said, "Of course."

Under the barrage, our house betrayed us, cracking and seeping at the foundation and leaking from above. We discovered our roof to be a sagging, disintegrating façade of substandard plywood. Hornets built a basketball-sized nest in our crawl space, and the stench of a maggot-filled raccoon rose from under the deck near our back door. The assaults arrive one after another and maybe they are not offenses against us, but simply life. Still, there is such a thing as too much.

The rot and decay in our house are a sickening metaphor for what is happening at work: the demolition of people. Emotional torture. Crimes against the state. Violations of human decency.

Such is the hard labor of living in a dream. Betrayal has startled me awake, my heart pounding, and as the harshness of that reality stings me like a chill-factor February wind, I hope my son, his blue eyes gazing innocently, does not detect my doubt. Even an island offers no insulation from human nature.

Hope is the surest pathway to disappointment. In this misadventure, disappointment has turned out to be a brief stop on the road to disillusionment. Our mirage transformed into a claustrophobic nightmare, and Grace and I have become barely visible to one another in the flat, low light of betrayal. Flawed expectations and frayed trust are as evident as the emptiness in our drawn faces.

I walk through the trees on a winding path to pass between worlds.

Clear Creek reminds me that the delicate truth about us is whispered by the water and the leaves. It's a secret easy to ignore in the march to campus or the rush home. Sometimes I still slow down to listen, but that seems just as foolish as chasing my mind to the office or to family. The not-listening is what takes time, and when the leaves fall and the water goes still I wonder if it is simply winter or if they have surrendered out of despair for my ignorance.

An island for my family has shrunk to this place that I alone occupy on my walks to campus—a space in which I can still hear echoes of my writer's voice, and I wonder if I could become light enough for the sound of water rippling in the creek to carry me to safety.

I spend most of my time now thinking about truth. The truth we tell to one another. The truth we tell ourselves. The truth that fills the void when no one can agree on what is real. That there is such a thing as a man with no deep well of joy, who may not have known it even as a child, but still hears echoes of what it must be like from within his soul, and that I might have knowledge of such a man.

I am alone. But I am not the only one. Even while I was mourning the death of my illusions, Grace watched her own sense of self fade in the bleak winter of Iowa, when even motherhood becomes susceptible to doubt. In her few moments of solitude, she slipped messages into bottles in search of a connection with someone, just to feel alive.

When I finally looked up to see her gazing out over the lonely ocean, I could only wonder the world she imagined, as the wind rendered my determined work into shifting, shapeless mounds. I felt betrayal, deep and hurtful. But there is a more powerful suggestion: that the betrayal is mine, and that it has been long in coming.

The consequences of my choices are beginning to accumulate. Inexplicable decisions. Unconscionable mistakes. The delusion of right action and the cowardice of inaction. They are stones pulling me down, knotting my shoulders and buckling my knees. We can throw off this weight by asking forgiveness, I'd been taught. But there is no going back to the beginning, to a starting place. Somewhere before fear.

And finally I am succumbing to the minor tragedy that unfolds from dreaming of a writer's life. I could not choose the path of artistic deprivation, instead seeking the benefactor of respectable employment to finance my life, hoping that some semblance of art would emerge in scant spare time. What a compromised life. Ultimately, I can measure lost opportunities only by degrees of separation as I begin the long surrender.

In my fifties, I have not published in a long while, nor have I spent much time in the company of writers—not that I have ever been very good company in that camp. I write, but the writing dream has gotten away from me, and like the body and brain of my youth, there may be no getting it back. Admittedly, my need to write has been a matter of emotional survival; I have never imagined an audience. To see my name in print has been my way of looking into a mirror to confirm that I actually exist. I don't know if I have the heart to look up and out for the next place and try to find some trace of myself.

Transition

STEADY AND LOW, with the entrancing subtlety of a meditative mantra, the voice of the mountains called. Reaching across the Great Plains and filtering through the chaotic noise of an entangled, distracted life, the calm tones carried a simple message.

Return, return, return.

Not to the place of my birth, or of my youth, or of any landscape I had lived in.

Instead, return to the deepest of dreams, to the basis of hope. To the heart of innocent aspirations. Return to believing in belief, and live within the enduring embrace of what had been a lifelong yearning. Breathe the deep, buttery scent of Ponderosa pines. Gaze up and out at the angular peaks of a spiritual ascent. Rise and remain above.

And when I was ready, and chose to listen, I heard it.

Grace and I, seeking unity through direction, gazed at a US map, opening ourselves to possibility, trying to find a place that would be the long-term home Iowa had failed to be. On a couch in our basement, we pointed, talked, imagined. We lifted a laptop off the coffee table and looked up some data until we found a disqualifier. Too hot. Too humid. Too many bugs. Too many people. Too expensive. Against these, we held up the principles of place—unmet aspirations for the life we imagined. These were spiritual measures not found in any database, and we struggled to express them. We expected to feel them rising up from within as a sense of belonging.

We thought we knew how that felt. The previous fall, we'd taken a family trip to Willis, Texas, to see my sister and my parents. It was our son's first major road trip—we'd made drives to Dubuque, Kansas City, Omaha, Chicago, Minneapolis, and Milwaukee, but none took longer than a day. This would be two nights on the road.

The landscape was new to all of us as we headed straight south through Missouri, then across Oklahoma into Texas. I took in what I could from behind the wheel, welcoming the changes in topography as they came, eager to add to my inner library of images and impressions. At certain points, I tried to draw forth our son's impressions. Mostly he was a man of one-word responses. But on Highway 19 through east Texas, on the way from Paris to Lake Conroe, we asked again what he thought of the area; after the previous day of smoke and haze from widespread wildfires in Oklahoma, we could finally see clear changes in our surroundings and wondered if he did, too. "They need to cut down all these trees," he said. "I can't see anything." Spoken like someone being raised in Iowa. Even with the woods across from his house, what he remembered while driving was the open fields disappearing at the edges into the midwestern sky.

Finally in Willis, where my parents and a sister's family live next to Lake Conroe, all of us could relax and embrace the illusion of being in another world, where our Iowa cares had no anchors in familiarity. And our deepest forays into that world came as excursions out on the lake on my sister's boat. Powering across the water, with the wind streaming through our hair, all three of us were transported—our only previous experience on the water had been on a rigid raft in the Chagres River along the Panama Canal, and we had possibly not been that relaxed since then.

At the helm, my brother-in-law was speeding to different areas of the lake in search of ideal spots to fish. He told us how the banks had become crowded with houses since his childhood, many of them grand and mansion-like with boat slips. I immediately lamented the development, but he mused about his memories without any visible regret; there was no sense of sadness in his voice. Besides, he was busy, for he knew the reference points below the surface of the water: two pine stumps over here, a brushy hole off the far point. Subtext. Not unchanging, but little changed in thirty years. A landscape he could trust, that he knew in the way that he knew his own interior self, and clearly, as he circled the boat, his eyes darting back and forth from the radar screen to a handheld GPS, he was searching with more—he was reaching down through the water, through memory and experience, with his spirit. He sought fish, yes, but he also sought something in the world that he could count on, and even before he learned if there were any fish to be had, he was reassured, at some level, that the hole was still there. Satisfaction is composed of such knowledge.

I longed for deep knowledge of a place I could understand in the way that he knew the bottom of the lake. I watched Grace gaze over the water and heard her sighs of longing. A place to explore and experience. To build bonds and memories. To bridge the formation of our son's life with our transition out of this realm.

Sitting in our Iowa basement that day, we knew Willis wasn't the answer. We'd visited during a narrow window of tolerance— mild weather, the bugs and snakes in remission. So we closed the map and agreed only that such a place must be out there.

Our map quests were also an exercise in reconnecting. We talked about what was important to each of us, including our young son. We wanted to get back to ourselves. To our original intent. For me this meant a place pulled from the dreams of my aspirational youth, when the sharp-edged Cascades and their thick pine forests taught me to imagine that a desert-dwelling boy stuck on the dry side of Washington State could find joy in his surroundings.

Yet most of my experience had been otherwise. I chased work and love across a harsh geography that refused to reveal my purpose or honor my landscape-inspired dreams. At each stop, illusion gave way to prickly reality. I may have been programmed to see it this way, being the child of environmental disaster from a place born of subsidized irrigation from dams that wrecked the rivers, sustained by a nuclear industry that left a poisonous imprint so profound that the place has become a boomtown of remediation.

Maybe, I reasoned, we are all the children of environmental disaster.

Still in the midst of our search, we decided to prove to ourselves we could control our quest for place. In the trough of the worst housing market of a generation, we put our house up for sale. Our logic was simple: if we happened to find the next place, and a way to get there, we didn't want to be anchored to real estate.

I sat on the couch with the map and the laptop. Closing my eyes halfway, I let the map search me. Find me, I thought. Find me.

After a few minutes, I flopped back and sighed. "Yes," I muttered. "I am this desperate."

So I searched. And my eyes fell on a familiar name: Flagstaff. I'd been there once for a writers conference, ten years earlier. All I could remember was pine trees, a vague upward slope leading out of town, and a long hike from the Northern Arizona University campus to a funky, old-style downtown. It was June, so the weather had turned warm, making the pines seem incongruous, and snow was merely a rumor.

And I remembered a night in the Spartan dorm room that I occupied. I sat cross-legged on my bed, a casement window open next to me to let in some cooler air, while I drank tequila from a brown ceramic bottle. It had been a gift, and I drank it as if on a vision quest, for I was among writers and trees under a clear mountain sky. Piercing stars cut through the warm, smooth layers of my tequila buzz, stirring my inner fears under the Milky Way. I felt exposed. Panic gripped me: a powerful conviction that someone or something was about to reach down from the night sky and snatch me up. Breathing quickly, I cranked the window closed, my hand shaking. I wasn't yet ready to rise up.

Later, I asked Grace about Flagstaff. Yes, she said, she'd been there, too. On a road trip. About ten years earlier.

As we planted the For Sale sign in our front yard, we wondered if it was possible that a place such as Flagstaff would be able to lift our spirits. And our son—had he already been unalterably influenced by the wide, manicured fields of Iowa and the idea that his neighborhood was a cultivated park? There was hope. His Waldorf preschool class made forays into the woods across the street, a stand of deciduous trees that on his scale must have seemed like a deep forest.

The fields and trees contrasted with the high desert of his birthplace in Reno, and as we contemplated our next move, I worried that our commitment to bringing stability into his life was resulting in the opposite. We left Reno because we chose not to stay. We were going to leave Ames because it was a failed attempt to stay.

Our house went on the market on a Thursday afternoon. After a flurry of showings and a few hours of negotiations, we accepted an offer on Sunday. Unbelievable. Impossible. But there it was. As we sat in the basement signing papers, our real estate agent asked us about next steps. I explained how our road atlas had been used as a seer stone, and how I searched the job listings at NAU and saw an opening. Within hours, I had applied. So, as I signed my name on yet another form, I told the realtor there was a possibility out there. But I felt as if I were lying a little. How could I call an application a tangible possibility? She looked at us as if we were insane.

But within a week, NAU called. In a few more days, a phone interview. Within two weeks, I flew with my family to Flagstaff. The moment we got off the plane at the airport, the flow of events made sense. Pine trees surrounded us. As we drove among them in our rental car, the San Francisco Peaks jutted into the northern horizon. The scene hearkened to my yearning for Northwest forests and deep memories of the Cascades.

Before the trip, I had read about how Flagstaff lies in the transition zone of Arizona, at the edge of the Mogollon Rim, a slice between sixty-five hundred and eight thousand feet in elevation that allows for expansive pine forests, tolerable summers, and snowy winters. Could it be a place that remained above change?

I knew the answer as I asked the question.

I had already begun to sense the movement from the fringes of middle age into something more defined and profound, more significant, as I passed across the boundary on my path to finality; a transition into the fullest understanding of limitations. Life decisions become easier when there's less resistance. I remember reading that once: "stop resisting." That doesn't mean to let life happen to you. It just means to live fully as life leads you in the direction of truth. Flagstaff felt authentic, even if—or perhaps because—it would mean less money, less space, less stuff.

I got the job. We moved.

Camping in a tent at the North Rim of the Grand Canyon, we marveled at our proximity to such a natural wonder, and not just that a side canyon cut into the earth fifty yards away. We talked about how the drive had only been a few hours, and that the south rim vantage point we could see across the way was less than an hour from home.

All of us were eager to know how it would feel to return to that home, itself in a place of mountains and trees. We'd camped locally a couple of times, kept up most of the night at one of the sites by bugling elk and yipping coyotes. There was an idea growing within us about altitude, about feeling above the rest of the world, even in the shadows of the peaks.

The sensation we anticipated found us as we climbed toward peaks on US 89. As we entered the realm of pines we rolled down our windows to breathe in the scent and remind ourselves that yes, we were home.

Even looking up at the peaks, we could not deny the influence of choices. We lived in a town home and counted ourselves lucky, knowing the local saw of "poverty with a view" meant outright hardship for many. And we harbor no illusions: we have arrived at a place that is already one of memory, where the local lore shovels feet of snow and throws open windows to easy summers. A place more of past than present.

The place is not ideal because no place is, but it reflects an ideal for a man with a life more than half lived. There's still time to fill a mind and heart with intimate knowledge of a place and mark each subtle shift. Time to consider the deep past and learn about what is here, now. To experience the aura of a monsoon storm and welcome the first drops, as satisfying as a good cry.

Unpacking What Cannot Be Saved

A SINGLE CHARRED OAK LEAF discharged from the sky settled peacefully onto our red cinder driveway, delivered by the updraft from flames five miles away as our lives sat in stacks of cardboard boxes, in transit once again.

Boxes stacked on the hardwood floor of a little house in Kachina Village. Boxes from the garage of our townhome; the same boxes we lived among, as if they were walls and tables and footstools, for about four months in an apartment on the east edge of Flagstaff. The boxes that delivered us from Iowa in pieces cushioned by packing paper and second-rate clothes, bound in haste with grim determination.

Now among the pines, they awaited release in a place we chose for rest and peace. A place to feel settled. But objects in motion driven by external forces tend to resist human intention. Life does not stand still, even if we wish to.

When the Slide Fire started on a Tuesday afternoon in May, it rapidly snaked its way north from Slide Rock State Park, along and up Oak Creek Canyon. Beautiful and popular West Fork, which we had hiked, lay in immediate harm's way. In my nearly three years in Flagstaff, I'd heard more than once that if a fire started in the canyon, Kachina Village would have no chance. And I had heard it recently, as the forest labored into spring with the parched breath of a desert, the image of rainfall a desperate mirage.

We moved here to experience life closer to the forest than to the city. Even in Flagstaff, referred to by Phoenix dwellers as "small" at seventy thousand people, the sense of city was encroaching on us like someone standing too close in a line. If we were going to live in the woods, then we wanted to live among the woods.

From the twelve-thousand-foot tops of the peaks, Flagstaff is merely an island in the pines. Kachina Village is a stepping stone. Most choose to be here not out of hubris—although multimillion-dollar weekend homes attest to the presence of ego—but for lifestyle. Dark skies. Quiet. Trees. This incursion into the interface was made thirty years ago by a developer, but it speaks to others who think like us, who want to see the Milky Way and hear squirrels skitter up thick Ponderosa bark, who want to drive into town for groceries or shopping of any kind. Seven miles separate us from the city, a stretch of freeway we would gladly negotiate for the freedom to glance over our shoulders and see jobs, errands, and tourists fading in the distance with waves of green ahead.

Just one day after the start of the fire, with not a single box yet opened inside the house, smoke billowed into piercing blue pools of sky serrated at the edges by Ponderosa crowns. From our front deck, I had to tilt my head back to take in a spectacle visible from space.

Through every online and word-of-mouth means we could find, Grace and I monitored the fire's progress, the irony of that phrase growing more biting by the hour. We quickly grew familiar with the symbols on the stock ticker of wildfire: acres burned, percent containment, number of firefighters deployed. We considered our range of options, leaning toward a conservative play. I took time off from work to rake the pine needles neglected for years by the property's previous occupants, and I did so fervently, filling twenty-seven bags in an afternoon. In the time my work cleared a theoretically defensible perimeter, more than three thousand acres surrendered to flames. Firefighters poured into the canyon. I thought of them, in my anonymity.

I learned that a public meeting was called for late that afternoon at the fire station a mile down the road. Still grimy from raking, I arrived at what might have been the set of a disaster-themed B-movie. Local residents streamed to a rec room being set up with microphones at a front table. All the metal folding chairs were occupied, people three-deep lined the sides of the room, and the back began to fill well beyond the posted capacity. Finally, someone at the front spoke. We were being directed to the open truck bay on the other side of the station. The crowd flowed out and around the building, people trying not to stumble over one another while vying for a spot and glancing up at the growing column of smoke.

After more delay, a county official began a scripted introduction, replete with thank-yous and acknowledgments. The bureaucratic parade was underway, the microphone passing from one elected official to another, as if we had hurried from work and home, many with children in tow, the threat of conflagration looming over us, to attend a campaign rally. Finally, the main speaker was introduced. He prefaced his remarks by saying the trigger point to any evacuation, voluntary or otherwise, would be if the fire reached Pumphouse Wash, a geographical feature that would serve as the open end of a funnel delivering flames to Kachina. As if distracted by pretense, he then waded through more scripted emptiness before delivering the non sequitur of the event. "And I received word just before our presentation started today that the fire has reached Pumphouse Wash."

Most ran; I sprinted to my car. Reaching home quickly meant negotiating those still afoot, especially the ones who had parked along both sides of two-lane Old Munds Highway. Horns honked, and taut lines of panic creased the faces of people struggling to reach their vehicles. After a half-dozen close calls with pedestrians, I arrived home to the eeriness of a place on the verge of abandonment, as if it could sense it was being left behind. Someone from down the street slowed as she drove past, calling from the window of her Jeep, "Were you there?" I nodded and she sped up toward home. Seconds later, I called Grace, who was in town. "We need to make some choices," I said.

She soon arrived with our son, and we crammed what we could into our two vehicles, wheeling from necessity to sentiment as we chose which box or which item was worthy of rescue: the fire safe, showing our lack of trust in its central attribute; my published writing; art posters designed by Grace; a plastic helicopter assembled by us for our son—to assure him, we reasoned, that its connection to childhood playfulness would sufficiently anchor his emotions during our exile. To assure us.

While we loaded our vehicles, a man in a khaki jacket declaring "Search and Rescue" on the back growled up to me on an ATV. He stopped long enough to say, "I'd leave if I were you."

We did not know where we would go. The next day would be our ninth wedding anniversary, and we had already decided, being cash-strapped from the move, that our house was our gift to one another. Now we hugged in front of it, unsure if the gift would last another day.

We wanted to say good-bye in some symbolic, meaningful way, but we didn't tell our son that. He already knew. I took pictures of him and his mother standing on the front deck. Their unsmiling faces were for emotional insurance, filed in a digital folder of dozens of photos hurriedly taken inside and out to form the basis of a claim, if all were lost.

Ultimately, after considering a few unsolicited offers, we spent the night in a guest room of acquaintances. We picked at the dinner they offered us and slept in the bed they made for us, unsure if we would return the next night or leave town. Or possibly return home.

On Thursday, the fire spread west into the Red Rock Secret Wilderness under the spell of back burn conjured by pyrotechnic sphere dispensers dropped from helicopters. But the army of fire-fighters stymied the flames at Pumphouse Wash, a place defended as a last stand. We debated our next move. Return, potentially needing to flee on a moment's notice? Impose upon our gracious, yet hardly known to us, hosts? Leave town? We talked, we agonized, we exhausted our already weary selves with scenarios. At a break in the dialogue, acceptance slipped into the void and settled upon us. We would return to our house. And we would unpack.

How much sense could be made of our lives if we were to lay out all the items contained in the boxes and bags of our two vehicles, and the few boxes that I had stashed in my office at work? Perhaps what we were willing to lose might offer a clearer idea.

We returned to the house because we felt prepared to leave it in a hurry, and destruction was merely a possible outcome, not imminent. No intention of making a last stand fortified us, not with a seven-year-old. So we agreed with a hug, peered at the smoky skies, and unpacked.

We ripped the tape from each box, the sound of its stubborn release from the cardboard the only disturbance in the house. Our son was at school. We did not talk. Instead, with silent focus, we pulled items from the boxes, reflecting in our isolation upon their meaning, even in the transience of the moment. What we extracted, what we placed in cupboards and on shelves, was what we could not save. If the fire turned, or the wind kicked up, or a spot fire jumped the line, this ritual of claiming space would be as empty as the charred frame that might be the outcome. And yet we persisted, box after box, unwilling to acquiesce to despair. If we were to have only a few hours of this place—home, now that it contained our material essence freed from the cardboard—then so be it. That's the memory we would have of it.

One by one we opened what remained—a majority of the boxes containing books—and placed our possessions for our stay, whether ten years or ten hours. The act of unpacking became an ongoing exercise in reflection and consideration far beyond the usual "Where should we put it?" Instead, we understood a little more deeply what each item meant to us, and that the material world is transient, uncertain, and unreliable.

In any move, there is always that sense of discovery even as familiar items are brought forth, but I was finding more than just what emerged from the box. I understood that I was putting into physical play the story that had been unfolding behind the veneer of work and family, the extraction of items, real and imagined, from the subconscious.

How often, in reflection, or meditation, or art, or psychotherapy, do we undertake this exercise, reaching into compartments of our minds, retrieving memories and experiences that may be abstract on their own, but when assembled or arranged constitute the story of who we have become. And when we pull them forth, then what? We can grow through the unpacking or simply find pleasure in retrieving the familiar. But there is also the resignation brought by age and affliction. At some point, most of what we have is long past, and re-handling any of it—such as the pain of lost love, or the exhilaration of finding it—only reminds us that the one thing we cannot save is ourselves. And for those whose unpacking is conducted in the darkness of depression or in manic frenzy, there is no certainty in what we uncover. We do not trust what we see, do not believe our perception to be reliable, except that everything seems broken, faded, fake. A lifetime of shoving regretful experiences into lost corners resists any call to disturb the monochrome stacks, which build all around until we are walled off from the world, from everyone.

Surrender and leave it all alone. Surrender and open everything.

Our actions put into play the motions of my mind, and those whose hands reached in to stir around and pull out the broken pieces. It could have been the crescendo of emotional events or the collapse of what held them together, but in the shadow of the mountain, in the midst of the forest, even before the fire had begun,

I sensed disaster smoldering from deep within. Long-lost dreams stirred, then reached out to awaken me, fear reverberating in my chest and lingering as dank humidity in my brain, and I breathed through the ozone of over-firing synapses. Once again, in my fitful sleep, I saw the warning—thick, tangled strands—before the nemesis. Shiny black, red hourglass blazing, always far bigger than in life. The black widow scuttles cunningly close. I evade, arms and legs filled with sand. My attempts to kill it, driven by mad intent, then desperation, fail. As the terror of futility grips me, a merciful force thrusts my awareness through a wall. I have flown outward and now I am up, gasping, never more deeply than the time, finally, the spider reached my hand and, suddenly transformed into a frothing black cat, tore at me with malice gleaming in its fangs.

Time for more bubble sheets. Many, many more. Filling in the blank spots to find answers. An algorithm to assign names to what cannot be seen or fully understood.

"We have your results," said the man with the degrees. "You scored quite high."

"In what?" I asked.

"In everything."

Unpacking is ceding control. It's accepting that we can own something, hold it, place it where we want it to be, all the while understanding that our actions could be overwhelmed by forces larger than we are. It's possibly even an act of courage.

At home, events confirmed our determination to be foresight. With each day, the threat diminished, although the fire eventually expanded to burn thirty-three square miles. The strategy to redirect it to an unpopulated area worked, but we mourned the loss of forest and understood that what had lain undiscovered to us in the Secret Wilderness would remain a mystery.

The defeat of the fire left us grateful and feeling fortunate, although full of grave respect for our choice of place. In Iowa, we had accepted the random rage of weather, but in Kachina we would be forced to admit we had placed ourselves deep in potential harm's way. We've since read plenty about the question of living in the interface—purely selfish, some writers claimed, as if choosing our home there was a moral failing—and wondered if our emotional attachments are simply more fuel for the destructive forces that could be wrought upon us. But they are attachments we are not ready to release, yearning as we did for a place that whispered to our spirits.

The fire has become part of our family's oral history, and on each drive through the canyon our son seeks the point of origin, asking as if it were a creation story—our lives in Kachina evolving from the spark that set off the blaze. Not quite a year later, we camped at Cave Springs in the canyon and visited Slide Rock for the first time. We took care with each step, holding hands, moving in unison across the waves and rivulets of smooth red stone. The creek flowed below and sunlight warmed our skin. We laid back, held within the heart of the place that could have destroyed us.

Safe.